To Jolie
love endures—
Kathleen
4·30·11

Sex After Death
a love story...

Kathleen Sterling

authorHOUSE®

AuthorHouse™
1663 Liberty Drive
Bloomington, IN 47403
www.authorhouse.com
Phone: 1-800-839-8640

First published by AuthorHouse 4/6/2011

ISBN: 978-1-4567-5585-0 (e)
ISBN: 978-1-4567-5586-7 (dj)
ISBN: 978-1-4567-5584-3 (sc)

Library of Congress Control Number: 2011904240

Printed in the United States of America

Any people depicted in stock imagery provided by Thinkstock are models, and such images are being used for illustrative purposes only. Certain stock imagery © Thinkstock.

This book is printed on acid-free paper.

Cover Photo: Teo Tamas

For Rodger

It's amazing how you can speak right to my heart
Without saying a word you can light up the dark
Try as I may I can never explain
What I hear when you don't say a thing

The old khaki jacket is frayed around the collar. One of its straps is hanging loose. The metal buttons that closed the front are tarnished and the wool lining is worn in places. The Field and Stream label is grey from years of rubbing against the back of a neck. Its various reporter's pockets are empty now.

It's been around the world and back. It smells of London, Paris, Prague and Rome. It carries the scent of a hundred trips and a thousand memories.

But mostly it smells like Rodger.

The jacket made its last trip home in April. I keep it under my pillow and make the bed around it. I lay in the dark every night holding it to me. Lonely, shaky and scared, I smell his smell and breathe him in.

I'm doubled over the jacket, holding on to this solid evidence that he was here.

This piece of him that was left behind.

Curled into a ball in the middle of the bed, I keen. Not mere crying, but wrenching sobs I pull deep from my chest, my legs, between my legs. Every part of me that loved him is aching with grief.

I cannot stop.

Alone in the house I let go. I will not show this face to anyone – friends, family, my daughter.

I cannot draw them into the pit of despair with me. I cannot let them see how deep the loss has cut through me, slicing me in two and taking part of me away.

With him gone, half of me is missing, and my body screams in pain from the amputation.

It is hours before there are no tears. I lay spent and exhausted, missing him, wanting him, needing him.

۶

Rodger walked into my life at four o'clock one afternoon.

Wrinkled khakis. Blue polyester short sleeve shirt. No sartorial star – but he had a twinkle in his eye and an easy smile.

I had called him on the recommendation of one of my employees. She had worked for him years before and talked about him constantly. We got tired of "Rodger this, Rodger that," and actually had Rodger jokes in the office about this paragon of newspaper virtue.

At a certain point, I took her seriously and called him.

I wanted to sell him my newspaper.

I was done.

Done with having started a business at twenty-two that I knew nothing about. Done with being twenty-five years old and trying to run a struggling enterprise. Done with employees, cash flow, deadlines.

I had no journalism background. I had an MBA in International Marketing, and a job offer in Paris. In my head I was already out of there.

On New Year's Eve, I'd broken up with my boyfriend of five years when I found out he'd been cheating on me the whole time with his slutty ex. I was done with men.

I was done with everything.

And then Rodger walked in. He heard my litany of arguments that he had the experience, he had the interest and he should buy the paper.

And he told me not to sell - but to hire him instead. He insisted I had a "tiger by the tail."

He was convincing, and he knew his stuff. He had owned his own paper for almost 30 years, had bought and sold three others, and helped start two more.

He sure convinced me. By 5 p.m. he was hired and I was hooked.

He was also hungry – as Rodger always was at five - so we stayed for dinner and more drinks. We talked non-stop for almost ten hours – about everything *but* newspapers. His ex-wife. My parents. His kids. Religion. Chamber gossip. My ex. Being single. Sex. Friends. They finally kicked us out at 2:30 am.

As we walked out he tossed a "see you later" over his shoulder.

I don't think so.

We had bared our souls to each other and I wanted more than that. Don't ask me what got into me. But I snapped my fingers and said "Sterling, come here." I grabbed this tall, good-looking guy and kissed him brainless right there in the parking lot. Then I walked away and tossed a "See *you* tomorrow" over my shoulder,

Driving home I knew I'd made the right decision. I knew it was right to stick it out with the paper and hire him.

I also knew that night I was going to marry him.

ॐ

Rodger already had an incredible history.

He was a small town Fresno boy whose father was both publisher of the local paper and the city's mayor. He was also President of California Newspapers Publisher's Association and Rodg and his brother met the many politicos who courted his father. Richard Nixon had breakfast in their kitchen while campaigning for his Senate seat.

Rodger started off selling advertising while getting a journalism degree at Fresno State. He spent time in the Air National Guard, loading bombs into planes. He loved to say that no one attacked Fresno when he was on duty. He kept the "raisins safe for the world."

Right after college he married, and they high tailed it out of Fresno for an ad exec job in Detroit. Always a car guy, he handled major accounts, working with Lee Iacocca, John DeLorean and other auto industry honchos. But the weather and distance got to them. They returned to California, but definitely not to Fresno. After another few years in the ad biz, an opportunity arose to buy the *Las Virgenes Enterprise* in Calabasas, a suburb outside L.A.

The weekly newspaper had been founded to bring water and

schools to the area, and once that was accomplished the owners put it up for sale. Young and callow but full of energy, Rodger took on the paper and Calabasas as well. He became Chamber president twice, founded a Pumpkin Festival, grew up with the town. In the '70s it was a sleepy place where horses still trod the main road.

The newspaper office was an old wooden building with a fireplace, where the staff would burn papers to keep warm in winter. Local businesses included a saddlery, some small restaurants, a real estate office, a silversmith and a few artists' studios.

Not the celebrity haven it is today, home to Britney Spears, Howie Mandel and the Kardashians, Calabasas in those days was surrounded by ranches and scattered small housing developments. But the *Enterprise* thrived, and Rodger made the most of it, focusing on local news, local development and local people - something he never strayed from in all his years as a journalist. He loved to say that, "Lousy local is better than wonderful wire."

He could talk to anyone, and did. I used to laugh and say he talked to presidents and paupers the same way. Straightforward, down home, good old boy. No pretense, no bullshit, just straight talk.

First off, he'd listen. He would lean forward in his chair, fold his hands, and really pay attention. Whether it was conducting an interview, listening to an old lady with a complaint, or humoring one of the many retired curmudgeons who hung around the office with gossip, political news and bad jokes, Rodger would give them his all.

When he sat down with Gerald Ford at the Marriott, he was the only one in the room with him. The former President was tired from the press trip, asked if he could "put his dogs up," rested his feet on a chair and talked for half an hour.

Rodger was easy going. He had all the time in the world. He made you feel like he really cared, because he did.

He loved people, and their stories.

One of my favorites was his friendship with Eddie Cannizzaro. "Eddie the Catman" they called him, because he rescued stray cats. Rodger met him doing a piece for the paper.

But Eddie had a back story. It was rumored that he was the triggerman who shot Bugsy Siegel for the mob.

Eddie and Rodg got to be coffee buddies, meeting regularly to catch up. One day Eddie actually talked about the old days. He said, "no one got killed who didn't need it." Bugsy had been stealing from Meyer Lansky, who ordered the hit. Eddie confessed to Rodger that he'd done it.

He'd shot Bugsy Siegal.

Years later, Eddie's obituary in the *Los Angeles Times* said the case was still open on the Beverly Hills PD books. It said that Eddie never confessed to the murders.

But he confessed to Rodg.

He told him the truth.

They all did.

He was friends with everyone from the local mechanic to television personality Bob Eubanks and politician Barry Goldwater Jr. He rode horses at Ronald Reagan's ranch while Reagan was campaigning for governor. He danced with Lana Turner at the old "Californian" restaurant, owned by Turner's daughter Cheryl Crane.

But he never lost his Fresno roots.

There was no guile about Rodger. What you saw was what you got.

A guy who loved to tell jokes, take time to have coffee, and somehow get around to writing it all down. He was one of the "nice guys," who supported his community, went to church when he could, knew everyone and befriended anyone who walked by.

He was truly baffled by his divorce, but devoted to his kids. He gave his ex everything but his car, sold his paper to the Hearst Corporation and moved one town over.

That's where I came in.

I was twenty-five to Rodger's forty-seven. I had run a company for three years, negotiated leases, bank loans and printing contracts.

I was mature for twenty-five, and he was ageless.

I was much thinner, blonde and busty. I was also in the newspaper biz.

I don't know which of those was more appealing - or if it was the fact that we just got each other right away. Rodg could make me laugh. We shared the same warped sense of humor of journalists - looking at the world with a skewed vision.

We both were avid readers. He read every newspaper and magazine he could get his hands on. I read books voraciously. We could sit for hours and just talk about world events, local politics, an idea, a joke, a story.

I could keep up with him. All of my siblings were educated, bright, and I like to think, terribly amusing.

As the oldest, I was the most responsible, the most pressured and the most guilt-ridden. We'd had a mixed up childhood. My mother was an artist and my first memories are playing on the docks in San Pedro while she painted. My father was an engineer who had a fanaticism for order. Sounds harsh, but it was also a childhood full of love and warmth that balanced out the criticism.

As the oldest, I wasn't allowed to date until sixteen - though my sister could at fourteen - by then mom and dad had loosened up. I had a group of friends I hung with all through high school. A late bloomer, it wasn't till my junior summer when I got a real "boyfriend." He was older - a college boy bent on medical school, and the nicest, sweetest guy you could meet. We had a year or so of heavy dating (no sex, remember I was Catholic born and bred) but then came graduation. He wanted to get engaged, and I was too young.

I ran the other direction - as fast as I could.

In college I was a little sister at two fraternities, had a blast, learned to drink and smoke. I dated, but still didn't sleep with anyone. I found out years later that one frat had bets on who would finally get me to bed. It wasn't either of them, though I did fall head over heels for an amazingly bright, sexy student with a British accent. It was unrequited love for four years and I shed many a tear over him.

I graduated from SC with a degree in Political Science and my virginity intact.

Up until then I just had other interests. I met Governor Jerry Brown, and spent many a Thursday night with my poli sci teacher, Brown and assorted Egyptian diplomats discussing the fate of the world - and watching them make trade deals. We even ended up at Linda Ronstadt's house in Malibu one night for a party. I met Madame Sadat, and Imelda Marcos. I was tuned in and turned on to working abroad.

I took a summer job after graduation at a law firm downtown to see if law was my thing, as I'd been accepted to the joint JD/MBA program at UCLA.

There I decided against law, but was determined to finally stop being the world's oldest virgin.

I met a young associate and we began hot and heavy dating. He was older and much more experienced. I was young, thin, and probably as hot as I'd ever get.

I actually lost my virginity on Good Friday, the day of fasting and abstinence. So much for Catholic indoctrination.

I also lost the urge the practice law. Halfway through my MBA I started the paper. The "official" press release says that my partner and I were prescient enough to see the burgeoning Warner Center as a growth market, which it was.

But truth be told, old college friends had hooked up at a party New Year's Eve, got toasted and confessed we hated our lives. One was a copy editor at a magazine. The other was working in an ad agency. I was still going to graduate school and not really inspired by the business courses. At that time if you were interested in marketing they told you to apply to department stores. Not my thing. In our bacchanalian fest, armed with the confidence that a lot of wine brings, we talked about starting a newspaper. We had the editorial, advertising and business ends covered. So we thought.

One of the three dropped out when he sobered up and realized he had a real job.

At the age of twenty-two, my partner and I each put $1500 each in the bank and rented an office. We were young enough and dumb enough to just knock on doors. We had a rate card, a plan, and no product. But there were enough people who believed in us to kick-start the paper.

After two years it was like a bad marriage - we were fighting about money, or the lack thereof - and editorial versus advertising space. We split up, and I kept the paper going.

My boyfriend had been editor of his college newspaper and lent a hand – and much advice. But when we broke up New Year's Eve I did it solo. Running the paper was difficult on my own, but I was involved in the chamber and the community.

It became something. It just wasn't my thing.

When an opportunity arose to sell TV syndications in Paris, I was ready to go.

But that was before Rodger.

Once he came to work we became inseparable.

Work was a joy, not a grind. We cranked it out all morning - laughing at story ideas, arguing over classifieds - working side by side to produce the paper. It's amazing how we worked in sync; he moved left, I went right, brushing up against each other. Small smiles, a pat on the back, a touch on the arm.

After a few weeks we couldn't take it anymore. After lunch we headed straight to his house and fell into bed. It was fast and furious - a desperate need to get closer than we had been all month. From that day on we couldn't keep our hands off each other. We made love every night, and almost every morning. We fell into each other and into love so fast and so deep.

Mornings at the newspaper were followed by long lunches and talk - always talk. I took him to evening chamber events where we'd grab something to eat, run home and barely make it to the bed.

Rodger liked to say he started out working for pay, and then went straight to "trade."

But we exchanged things other than bodily fluids.

He loaned the paper money. I gave him a check for child support when the Hearst payment was late. The boundaries became blurred and then nonexistent.

We worked, played, slept together 24/7. We never stopped talking. We never stopped being fascinated by each other.

He was a morning person. I'm a night owl.

He slept with the windows open. I sleep under two comforters.

He drank red. I drink white.

His pillow was hard as a rock. Mine is a soft little down ball.

His car was tuned to talk radio. I listen to news or classic rock.

He loved Nascar. I had season tickets to the Hollywood Bowl.

Rodg believed you could spell a word more than one way. I straighten everything on the paper.

He hated holidays. I live for Christmas.

He cried when things went right. I cry when things go wrong.

He loved staying in. I love going out.

Rodg was a strong conservative. I'm middle of the road.

He was an indifferent Presbyterian. I'm a strong Catholic.

He was a World War II historian. I'm a trashy novel queen.

He drove a sedan. I drive an SUV.

He graduated college in '59. I was born in '59.

We were a perfect match.

Everyone loved Rodger.

Everyone *except* my family.

They wanted to have me drug tested.

They didn't understand how their perfect virgin daughter (!), straight-A student, former debutante, who'd been accepted to UCLA Law School, the London School of Economics and SC Law, business owner and young entrepreneur, could hook up with this old guy.

He had no job, was divorced, not Catholic, and had four kids.

They made my life hell. The only snag in our relationship came from my side of the family. My grandmother disowned me, and my mother cried her eyes out and was convinced Rodger was there to steal the newspaper. Not that there was much to steal. I tried to sell it, remember? But they didn't get it. They didn't get to know Rodger, and that was part of the problem. I had brought him to the house a few times until they understood that he was more than a business associate. Once they figured out I was sleeping with him they were apoplectic.

And they didn't let up.

They drove by my house to see if I was there. They called constantly to find out what I was doing, and with whom. They were relentless, and it was ridiculous. I was a grown woman with my own life.

But I'd always been the perfect oldest child.

I didn't really drink or do drugs. I'd been the oldest living virgin. I'd done everything right and had always been the responsible one of the family. But they didn't trust my judgment.

They didn't see beyond his stats. They didn't see that he'd sold his paper to for half a mil. They didn't see that he was a great father. They didn't see that he was my best friend, first and foremost. We came together and nothing could keep us apart. Even my family.

I had to choose and I chose Rodger.

I loved him that much.

He meant that much.

He was that much.

I met my father away from the house one day and issued my own ultimatum. "Either call off the dogs or you'll never see me again," I told him. One of the hardest things I ever had to do was confront my family. My dad stood up for me, because he believed that I would leave.

Though they didn't warm up, they did back down.

I never looked back. No one was going to come to our wedding. My parents didn't pay for it. I didn't care. I had found the person I wanted to be with for the rest of my life. It was a watershed moment, and I grew up even more.

Years later, my mother told me I had the best relationship in the entire family.

I already knew that.

Our first trip together almost wasn't.

Rodger had a client in Costa Rica – a former colleague who was building a resort. He was a burnt out stockbroker from San Francisco with too much money and too many bad habits. He was told to get out of the rat race or die.

So he bought four hundred acres of virgin land and set out to build his dream.

He invited Rodg down to write about it, and offered to pay for my ticket as well. At the time, my parents were still crazy. So I didn't want to rock the boat.

But damn! I wanted to go. Rodg was persistent. He showed up on the way to the airport and said, "I still have your ticket."

Literally throwing my destiny in with his, I tossed a bathing suit, my passport and money in my purse, locked the door behind me and followed him.

Story of our life together.

I told my parents I was going with a girlfriend, and we took off on a dream vacation.

There were only five of us on the whole property and we had our own thatched roof cottage. We were told not to wander out at night, as there were jaguar on the beach and snakes in the jungle. We snuggled together in this primitive, sexy place, took the advice and stayed in bed.

We swam under waterfalls. Found little rock ponds to splash in. Lived on fish, fruit and tropical drinks with native rum. Paradise.

During the day we'd wander away from the main camp. Like Burt Lancaster and Deborah Carr we made love one afternoon on the beach with the waves just kissing our feet. Rodg buried the condom deep in the sand and years later would joke to me, "there's some fish out there with my face!"

We would return two more times to Costa Rica, but none was as brilliant as that first, illicit, wonderful trip where we got to know each other far away from the madding crowd.

It stands to reason we weren't allowed to marry in the Catholic Church.

The priest told us because Rodger had been married in the Presbyterian Church to another Presbyterian, it was a valid marriage. If he'd married a Catholic in the Presbyterian Church, it wouldn't have counted.

Semantic bullshit.

A woman I know was married a week after that discussion, on the altar, with four priests attending. Her husband's daughter from his previous marriage was the flower girl. It's not what they say, but whom you know.

He pressed Rodger to get an annulment. Even my mother was in on that argument. He refused. Refused to invalidate his last marriage. Said, "I won't make my children bastards."

He and I were disgusted, and went over to the community church.

Since my parents weren't contributing, it was a "do it yourself." We kept it simple, but beautiful. The church had a stained glass window and the sun shown down on our day in glowing colors. We didn't need anything but each other. In reality, we should have saved the money and eloped.

But we wanted to share the day with our good friends. Celebrate us. Acknowledge our commitment. Validate our love.

My sister relented and made my wedding dress as her gift. My parents, ironically, gave me a list of their friends to invite. One said she wouldn't come to the wedding because we weren't getting married in the Catholic Church, but had the gall to come to the reception. My dad insisted we have a full bar - but we could only afford beer and wine for the two hundred invitees. He finally broke down and wrote a check for the booze.

In retrospect, I don't know if they were cruel, or just confused. They didn't know what to make of us and didn't know how to handle the situation. Whatever.

The wedding itself was a blur. I cried all the way through it because I was so happy to be marrying Rodger. I was also overwrought from the emotion of fighting my family and relieved just to have made it to this day.

We had our reception at a beautiful little restaurant. Everything was pink and green and very French. The whole family came, and my father and brother sang with the violinist. Everyone danced at my wedding. It was a turning point. Basically, we were a done deal and they had to get used to it.

I have only flashes of memory. Vignettes from the day. I just wanted to get it over with and start my new life. To this day I haven't scrapbooked any of the photos. I've put it on hold. Don't want to relive the stress.

We left the restaurant at the end of the night and went to the hotel. That I remember. We 69'd each other and basically rubbed each other's feet. No sex. We were exhausted from the emotion, the ordeal, the day.

We took off for Napa the next morning, and had an incredible honeymoon up and down the California coast. We stayed at little out-of-the-way hotels. Ate well, drank lots of wine, made love morning and night, clung to each other.

Our life together had begun.

"Come fly with me" was the theme song of our marriage.

Travel was our raison d'etre. Our escape. Our not-so-guilty pleasure.

Part of it was easy because of the newspaper. PR people gave journalists free trips if we wrote about the destination. You think?

We would get the itch every third month or so if we hadn't gone away, somewhere, anywhere. We were escaping the stress of deadlines, family, money pressures.

We really didn't need an excuse.

We just went.

The best times of our lives.

We'd squirrel away cash until we had enough. Rodg was great at saving money from the office. He had an old Sterling Bank deposit bag where he'd keep our mad money. We'd wait for a great airfare and then take off. His favorite thing was to say, "Let's go!"

Sometimes we really couldn't afford it. But we knew we couldn't afford not to. My parents had money but bad health. They never traveled when they could have, and we didn't want to end up like that. Rodger used to say "let's piss it away now and have a good time." So we did.

Unencumbered by work pressures, we traveled the world like carefree sprites. Paris was our second home. It sounds pretentious but we spent so many vacations there we knew it like our own neighborhood.

These were never expensive trips – we stayed on Rue Cler in our favorite little boutique hotel. We took long walks all over the city. Visited museums, walked the Champs Elysee, stopped at little cafes. We packed picnics from the market stalls – a bottle of wine, cheese, bread, fruit, pastries. We sat on a little bench on the Champs de Mars and watched people. We spent lazy afternoons making love in the tiny garret room overlooking the Eiffel Tower.

We had a deal. Everyone knew when they traveled with us there was something for the guys – and something for the girls. So much war history with Rodger, then I got to shop.

I remember walking the beaches of Normandy. The fog was in and it looked like the troops had just left. From Paris to Poland we did museums, battle sites, concentration camps and more.

The war stuff was actually fascinating. I learned so much about what Rodg call "w.w.i.i." by visiting the Cabinet Underground War Rooms in London. Auschwitz. The Holocaust museum in the south of France. Shindler's factory in Krakow. Recreation of the blitz. We did it all and loved it all.

And then there was shopping. I'm addicted to flea markets, and have a plate fetish. The two go hand in hand. So Saturday mornings Rodg would either accompany me or let me trot off to the nearest sale. His only rule was "you buy it, you carry it." That worked well for a while until I bought so much I had to have help – or stash it in another suitcase. He never really got upset until he forbid me to buy the 120-piece place setting of china on our last trip to Paris. I did anyway – it was a steal. He really didn't talk to me for a whole day. But I won him over that night.

One year we just needed to get away. Work was tough. Life was stressful. So we headed to Paris with no agenda. We did nothing for a week. No tourist stuff, No museums. On our return my friend asked me what I saw that I liked best.

I said, "the ceiling."

Rodg was a package deal, and came with four children.

At twenty-five years old, what I knew about raising kids was limited to my experience with siblings. Not much help.

The little guys, as I called them, were only nine and ten at the time. To say I was somewhat intimidated would be an understatement.

The older two were nineteen and twenty. I barely passed them on the maturity scale.

But they were - and still are - amazing.

I fell in love with them right away. They were bright, funny, inquisitive little people in their own right. And they were Rodger's. They were as much a part of him as the newspaper, his sense of humor, his Fresno roots. He was first and foremost a father and a family man who adored his kids.

Love him. Love them. It was easy.

I never tried to replace their mother - I couldn't. First of all, I wasn't that much older. Second of all, that wasn't my role. I wasn't there to judge, to scold, to parent.

But I was their friend.

I taught them table manners by telling them that when they got interested in girls they should know the proper way to hold a fork and knife. I bought them cool clothes. Rodg was a "Disneyland dad" and we'd always dream up fun things to do.

The four of us were together constantly, as Rodger had custody every other weekend.

My family didn't get it.

Why would I take this on?

I tried to explain that I loved it. That we had fun. That the little guys were a joy. That Rodg lit up every time we went to pick them up. They were a part of his life, so they were a part of mine.

The older kids were more leery. They'd lived through the reality of the break up and had heard the charges leveled on both sides. They knew how bad it had been and were skittish of anyone new.

I don't blame them.

I came into the picture late in the game. They had had a family. They had a mother. They had a father, and a pretty stable life until the divorce. Then their father moved out, and got a much younger girlfriend.

I can only imagine.

I made it a point, and to this day have never wavered, about not criticizing their mother. Of not talking about the divorce. I only got one side of the story - their mother had another. Rodg admitted that his first mistress was the newspaper, and that he could have paid more attention to the home front. But he was young, ambitious and building an empire. He was a terrific provider and a great dad.

They lived in an amazing house off Malibu Canyon, which after the divorce they sold to Diane English, the producer of the "Murphy Brown" TV show. They owned a cabin in Cambria by the Pines, a beach house in Ventura, and a vineyard in Fresno.

This was all what we called "BK." Before Kathleen.

When Rodg moved out he left all the furniture, all the property, and all the memories to the kids.

We met three years later, and began building a relationship with each other, then with them.

Over the years they have come to visit, to stay. They call, they write. We are a family. The entire gang comes every Christmas. I put on a big deal, with presents filling the living room. Fill the "bag o'crap" (our version of the stocking). At the paper we get tons of promos. New videos. Really bad CD's. Movie specialties like a first aid kit for the movie "Nurse Betty" or umbrellas for a Bond movie. Water bottles from 10K runs.

Socks. They're big on socks.

I stuff the bags with them. When the oldest turned forty I stopped. Our worst Christmas ever. They couldn't believe I'd break tradition. No one had bought socks that year, knowing they'd be in the bag. So it continues.

They're still my kids. I'm still the wicked stepmother. They call me constantly. We meet for drinks.

I love them all. They are my kids - you better believe it. You don't have to birth someone to belong to them. They were Rodger's - and now they're mine.

We cling to the notion of family.

The one they have, and the one we've built.

Katie was conceived in Venice.

She's always embarrassed as hell when we tell anyone, but to me it's wonderful. We were at our best when traveling.

Before we got married, Rodger agreed to have another child. He was devoted to his older kids and didn't want to upset the apple cart, but knew it was important to me.

Since many of my friends had trouble getting pregnant, I figured it would take a while. We'd kick off our first attempt with this trip.

If nothing else, we'd have a lot of fun trying.

We left for Italy in early March. They were glorious days of ancient ruins, good food, and "liquid sunshine," our guide's euphemism for our daily glass of wine. We were blissfully happy, touring all day and making love all night in narrow, funny beds.

Good Catholic girl that I was, it must have been two weeks into the trip when I was sick as a dog.

The funny thing was that Rodger kept watering the flower boxes outside our hotel window. Even at home he never let me throw out dead or dying flowers. He couldn't stand seeing wilted plants.

I found out I was pregnant the minute I got home.

Evidently he brought more than flowers to life that trip.

Atta boy!

That night, Rodger won every award they could think of.

"Way to Go." "Special Achievement." My favorite: "Outstanding Performance."

He got accolades, catcalls, slaps on the back.

He was surrounded by his peers, and they applauded him.

It was a long trip back to Fresno, and I was along for the ride.

It was Rodger's 35th high school reunion. Many of his friends had retired. Some had divorced. Most had stayed in Sanger. A lot had grandchildren. All had grey hair.

Rodger had a 30-year-old wife who was seven months pregnant.

All hail the conquering hero.

We weren't crazy sex addicts.

We were just crazy about each other.

We couldn't keep our hands off one another. We were both so ready at this stage of life to be loved, and to give love – and that was the best way to express it. We could laugh together in bed. We could spend hours on each other. Given the choice between bed and … whatever, we'd usually fall into bed.

In the beginning of the relationship it was every night and every morning. We were young(ish) and in love. We didn't have a lot of money, but we had time. And we spent it wisely. We were also free with no one else at home.

When Kate came along it only made us love each other more.

Look what we created, Rodg would say.

Look at what love made.

So much of this sounds too intense. Not real life stuff. But it wasn't intense to us – not every moment.

We just lived and breathed and completed each other.

Much though, was day-to-day life. Kids, work, family, money.

But the foundation was always there. We were always a team. A couple. One half of the other. So he always had my back – and I his.

Not that we were perfect, but we didn't argue. Didn't fight. Thursdays at the paper were legendary for their squabbles but we managed to have only one fight a year, and it was a big one. We blew it all out over one or two days. Money, kids, ex-wife, parents – all the stresses. Since my Fresno boy didn't like to fight it was over almost as soon as it started.

Though we lived a fairy tale romance we weren't always the Prince and Princess Charming.

I'd get bitchy, he'd get tired. He got pissed at my shopping, I got frustrated at how he ruined the laundry.

We were a normal married couple, who just happened to stay in love.

Rodg was a hopeless romantic.

He'd cry in movies when things went right. He'd always say, "I love you."

But he was an abysmal gift giver.

He'd panic at holidays and birthdays. He worried about pleasing me or disappointing me.

Part of it was me. I loved to shop, to choose the perfect gift, every time.

Part of it was Rodg. He was just clueless.

He gave his first wife a box of hangers for Christmas one year.

"Hangers?" I asked him.

"She was always complaining about the hanger lines in her clothes. So I went to J.C.Penny and got her nice ones."

Then there was the year I opened the card and there was a hand-drawn picture of a horse.

"And?"

"They're horseback riding lessons."

I'd never expressed an interest in horses. I'd never ridden one while dating Rodger. At Girl Scout camp my horse had fallen over with me atop him.

Not the most inspired gift.

Rodg did best when he was spontaneous. After seeing a movie at the mall he marched me over to a jeweler to buy me a pearl choker, just like the one the heroine had been wearing in the movie.

He loved having me pick out something. There he was like a kid in a candy store. "Do you like these? This one? How about this?"

He was tickled pink when I wore it. And so proud.

I'd show him what I'd chosen and he'd duck his head to the side like a little kid. Like "ah shucks."

And he knew he'd done good.

It's my favorite room in the house.

The library.

Because if there's one thing writers do, it's read. The books were getting out of control. We had nowhere to put them.

It used to be the "guest" room. But we had guests stay over few and far between, and when they did, they tended to stay for months. We had to change that.

I had floor to ceiling shelves built in, and painted the rest of the room red. Found great fabric with big Roman style letters, and covered a deep, oversized, antique chair I found at an estate sale.

It became Rodger's haven. A warm, cozy room filled with books, his school mug, pictures of his mom, his kids, me. Funny things we'd picked up in our travels - a clay pot from Costa Rica, a stuffed camel from Egypt. The three baseball hats he'd wear, depending on the game - Fresno State for him, UCLA for his oldest, USC for me.

I filled the front shelves with the antique books from my grandmother. Gorgeous and very library-esqe.

But it's the titles on the other shelves that told who we were.

A floor to ceiling section of World War II - everything from the four volumes of Churchill to Ike, Wolfpack, Hitler and more Hitler. Rodger's passion, and he'd read every one.

My book club books, on their own shelves, showing the depth and breath of our selection - from Tolstoy to Steinbeck to Nora Ephron. The shelf of children's books.

The travel books, spilling over three long shelves, put in sideways, on top of each other, crowding each other, told the story of our journeys, our dream vacations, our plans.

One shelf holds one of my favorite pictures of Rodger. He's sitting in a hotel bathtub with his glasses on, reading the *London Times*. The paper covers him from thigh to chest, and it's just a great grab shot.

There's a place for our yearbooks, our photo albums, the chronicles of our lives.

One wall holds a collage of what's important to us. The drawing his son made of the old newspaper building. The letter from Reagan thanking Rodger for his support. A portrait of Ike that my brother gave him. The pen and ink of the old Calabasas wagon, signed from the artist "to the fastest pen in the west."

The list of "62 Things You've Already Done" I made for Rodg on his 62nd birthday.

The room is all him, and all his.

Here, he writes out the bills. Reads quietly in the early hours of the morning. Writes letters to his friends. Writes editorials for the paper.

The desk holds a picture of me in a silver frame. A picture of Kate in her school uniform. A picture of Rodg and the kids in Paris, holding a baguette and a bottle of wine.

The library is a collection of great books, but more importantly, it's a collection of great memories.

"62 Things You've Already Done" was one of the best things I ever did.

Playboy did a piece on "50 Things You Need to Do by 50," and Rodg read it to me. His birthday was coming up, and what did he really need? He wasn't into clothes, had way too many war books, and we'd already booked a trip for April.

So I stole Hef's idea, and wrote up sixty-two things Rodg had already done in his lifetime.

It was an impressive list.

Things he had done over the course of his life that meant something. To him, to me, to the family, to the community.

Fun stuff – Danced with Lana Turner. Owned over 30 cars, Made love on a beach.

Cool stuff – Nixon, Reagan, Ford. A mobster.

Family stuff - Raised five kids. Married a younger woman. Assisted at his child's birth. Rode motorcycles with his boys. Hugged his kids.

Funny stuff - Raised chickens. Slept in his car (after a fight). Owned a "herd" (one cow).

Business stuff - Owned five newspapers. Became a millionaire.

Started over. Owned a vineyard. Owned a ranch. Sold his newspaper. Restarted it six years later.

Travel stuff - Climbed the pyramids. Skinny-dipped in the jungle. Stayed at three of the top ten hotels in the world. Went through the Panama Canal. Rode a horse through the rainforest. Took every kid to Europe.

Young stuff - Played football. Voted Rainbow Girl's sweetheart. Outran the cops.

Rodger stuff - Wrote his own column. Had his own jokes told back to him. Published under a pseudonym. Cooked a mean steak.

Lived long enough to collect Social Security.

And my favorite.

Learned that love is really lovelier the second time around.

A horse walks into a bar. The bartender asks, "Why the long face?"

It was one of Rodger's favorite jokes for his column. He wrote "The English Channel" in all his papers, filled with bad puns, shaggy dog jokes, anecdotes, word play and more.

It was everyone's favorite part of the paper.

We could have hard-hitting news on the cover. Medical marijuana busts. Death of a community leader. Fire. Earthquake. And still people would come up to us and say, "I loved the joke about..." Often people would tell him a great joke they'd just heard so he could put it in the column, not realizing they had actually just read it there.

Readers would say, "I like that English guy." Now Rodg really isn't English. He started the column way back in the dark ages when there were only a few television channels. So he basically created his own, and named it thus.

He would always use his friends as pigeons. Jerry Humes tells the one about the rabbi and the giraffe. Jeff Heller writes in to ask the difference between a shoemaker and a cobbler.

They all got a kick out of it. Instant celebrity on a small scale – as people they knew would then say, "I read your joke in the paper!"

Once in a while he'd put in something a little risqué, just so, he said, "I can check that people are still reading."

But they were. And sending us new material all the time.

Lawyer jokes from lawyers.

Kid jokes from Katie and her friends.

It was a community affair.

It made people laugh, and did for damn near 50 years.

It started out as a beautiful weekend.

Rodg and I drove to Big Bear on Friday morning, earlier than the rest of the gang, just to have some time alone.

We arrived about 2 p.m. and went to rest after the drive. We got to our room, looked at each other, and just dove in. It was one of those times we just laughed, tore our clothes off, rolled around on the floor, made it to the bed. We made love for the next hour in every position we could. Holding each other, we finally got our nap, and woke up when the rest of the family came up the mountain.

We had a nice dinner, slept well and the next morning took our favorite walk along the lake. Quiet talking, holding hands, gossiping about the kids, work, nothing serious, just chatting. Rodg went to watch news on T.V. while the girls went to the flea market. He stayed there on and off all day, joining us for lunch, looking and shaking his head at what I'd bought.

Dinner Memorial Day weekend is always at the Captain's Anchorage, where we host the "Manhattan Memorial." It's prime rib and a couple of Manhattans in honor of my dad, as this was his favorite place. Afterwards we settled in to watch a movie, and Rodg went to bed early. Big Bear is at 7,000 feet and we all get tired in the mountain air.

After the movie I snuggled down next to him and fell asleep.

At 2:30 a.m. I awoke to the headboard banging against the wall. My first thought was "Damn my sister! She's always moving the furniture around." I said something like that to Rodg and he mumbled. It kept banging, and Rodger kept mumbling.

"Wake up honey, you're dreaming."

He didn't stop making noise.

I shook him. "You're scaring me. Wake up."

I was still half asleep but worried. I panicked then, jumped out of bed and turned on the light.

"Oh my God."

"God."

"God, no."

He was struggling to rise out of bed and one half of his face was drooping. I screamed down the stairs, "Rodger's had a stroke. Get Stephen! Get Stephen!"

My baby was trying to move. Trying to get up. He knew something was wrong but couldn't do anything.

I think I froze in place for half a minute.

My brother Stephen, a doctor, was there in seconds. He knelt on the bed and calmed Rodger down. Checked his vitals. Looked at me to confirm it was a stroke. On his way up he'd yelled to my sister to call 911 and get an ambulance.

They took forever to get there.

We could see them from the upstairs window, struggling to find the house and turning the wrong way down the street.

I don't remember much except thinking, "I have to get dressed."

Katie came up the stairs, followed by a shocked family, and stood there until we held hands and said an "Our Father" around the bed, around my guy, waiting for the paramedics.

There was nothing else to do.

Because of the narrow stairs they had to take him down on a chair. He put out his good hand to push back from the wall. "That's a good sign, Steve, right?" I begged.

We all huddled around the ambulance as they loaded him. "I need to go with him," I cried as I held his hand.

They wouldn't let me. They wanted to airlift him straight to Palm Springs and a major hospital, but didn't know which one. My brother John followed the ambulance to the airport and said he'd call us.

Steve, Kate and I drove down the mountain in silence. It was two hours to Palm Springs. Two hours not knowing what hospital we should go to.

Two hours where Rodg was alone without me.

Two hours without him.

Two hours not knowing if he was alive.

John finally called and told us they airlifted him to Desert Memorial. We decided at 4:30 a.m. to call his daughter so she could tell the boys.

At the hospital Rodger was still in the ER.

They wouldn't do anything for him.

They couldn't do anything for him.

"What about the miracle drug for strokes?" I pleaded and begged to no avail. Because he was already on Coumadin, a blood thinner, they couldn't give him more or he'd bleed out. Stroke drugs are just heavy-duty blood thinners. They also couldn't verify the exact time of the stroke and this stuff has to be administered within three hours. "But it was 2:30 a.m.," I kept saying. They told me that it could have happened earlier, that's just when I woke up.

I was trapped in a ring of protestations, doctors in and out, all telling me the same thing, "We can only monitor him."

My guy, my life.

There in the bed.

And nothing anyone could do.

I remember looking at him lying there and thinking irrationally they'd cut off his favorite shirt. Like that mattered.

They finally moved him upstairs, and that's when the real nightmare began.

ॐ

Rodg – a good day used to mean good cash flow.

A good day now, on day four of this roller coaster ride, means you squeezed my hand, opened your eyes or have a low blood pressure reading.

How things change in an instant.

I love you more than ever before, and am your fierce guardian at the hospital. Sleeping by your side I'm obsessed all night by the monitor reading your pulse, respiratory and BP numbers.

The weird thing is I keeping thinking, "I've got to tell Rodg this," or "I can't wait to tell Rodg."

But I can't.

That's you in the bed.

You who had the stroke.

You – my life partner and best friend I can't share this with.

I can't tell you the tough parts – the fear, the panic, the feeling of impotence with arrogant doctors.

I can't tell you about the great nurse who got – finally - nutrition into your IV. Or how funny it was when I asked if you hurt and you covered your crotch.

I can't tell you how scared I am that we almost lost you. Or the absolute cold throughout my body as you were loaded into the ambulance. The deal I made with God on the awful ride down the hill that I wouldn't drink wine anymore if you lived...

You're there in front of me –but I can't tell you all of this.

I can fight the doctors for pain meds. I can watch over you like a fierce mamma lion, but I can't share any of this with you.

I keep reminding myself of three things – alive, awake and aware.

The first time you squeezed my hand was like giving birth all over again with all the joy.

Steve keeps telling me it's baby steps.

I so desperately want to believe him.

The first stroke pretty much robbed Rodger of speech. He didn't get to tell me that he loved me, if he hurt, how he felt.

He couldn't talk, but he could still communicate.

The first few days when he was still somewhat aware of what was going on, we asked him questions. I desperately wanted to get a response, to know he was still cognizant.

He would squeeze my hand if he understood, or wanted to say yes. I pushed harder than I should have sometimes. I just wanted to believe he was okay, he was there, he was getting better.

On one of those days my brother was with me, flexing Rodg's hands and talking to him. He was responsive, and we were hopeful.

He still didn't speak, but was more alert than usual.

Steve asked him some questions, then out of the blue asked him, "Who do you love more than anyone?"

Rodg didn't hesitate. He picked up his arm - no small feat - and poked me in the side. That he could muster that effort was in itself amazing. But that he also knew where I was in the room was everything.

He didn't need to speak.

He didn't ever need to speak again.

He told me with that touch everything I needed.

I knew already. But it was nice to hear it again, however he said it.

46

The night Rodger had his second stroke, they told us this was the end.

We each took our private time with him. He was fading fast, slipping away from consciousness.

That amazing brain, that quick mind, that funny guy of mine, was going.

He never got to say goodbye. There were no last words, no emotional farewells.

But I had my moment. I made it quick, knowing that I would stay with him all night after the others left.

He would not be alone.

I came in, talked to him, and lay across his stomach.

His good arm came up around me and stroked my back. He was comforting me. I don't know if he knew the end was near, or if it was just reflexive.

But for a few moments, I got him back.

I got to be held.

I could pretend.

Could pretend I was taking him home.

Could pretend we *were* home.

For those few minutes, it was just the two of us, as we always were. My holding onto him, him holding tightly.

I'd give anything to get those five minutes back.

My love.

I can't help you and it's killing me.

You've left your body and have gone on to that better place.

But that beautiful body that I loved so well –and so often – is trapped. Stuck in a coma. Never in a million years did I expect this.

We actually prayed for a happy death. I made sure you were in no pain, no distress. Prayed we *would* get the midnight phone call everyone dreads.

But it never came. "His condition is the same," said the nurse.

So now what, my love?

I thought telling them "do not resuscitate" was the worst. But this is a living nightmare. I don't know what is going on behind those closed eyes. They say you are deep into it and have no cognition of any of this. I pray that is so – I would die if I thought you hurt at all.

Are you were scared, not knowing what was happening to you, in pain or worse?

I'm the one now scared and not knowing.

Today could still bring release. I'm going to talk to the doctor. Your body is shutting down – and this sounds awful – but I hope it fades peacefully.

Our friend Danielle showed up with paint and brushes to take your handprints. She made a set for each child and grandchild.

Your beautiful hands that I've had all over me, are now preserved for me to have always.

And last night was your real memorial.

All the kids and I got very, very drunk - talked about you for hours.

They will miss their dad so much.

They love you so much.

The stories they remember, the things they love about you, the things their friends said about you.

I hope you were listening.

We shared your life, with the people who love you the most. I don't think either of us ever realized the depth of their devotion.

I hope you heard.

I hope you know.

They needed to say it – for themselves and for each other.

Oh baby.

We're letting you shut down.

We've taken out most of the tubes, bells and whistles, stopped the intrusions. Stopped the meds that will only prolong the inevitable.

After each child said their goodbyes Wednesday night we opened a bottle of your favorite Merlot. Said a prayer. Put a little wine on a cotton swab in your mouth.

And toasted the most amazing man we'd ever known.

ॐ

The day Rodger died I was alone with him all afternoon.

My beautiful boy.

I had to touch him one last time – that tall, gorgeous body. He had no tubes in him, no wires. Just my guy.

I ran my fingers through his silver hair. Put my hands on his face, rubbed my favorite spot where rough beard meets smooth cheekbone. Kissed his eyes, his mouth. Splayed my fingers over his chest hair and for the last time grabbed hold.

I stroked down his arms and placed our hands palm to palm – those big hands that held me, held Kate, touched me, touched so many. Hands that were so strong and so gentle.

I stroked his stomach, his thighs. Closed my hand on his penis, which lay there full and strong.

He never moved, but it was enough for me to see and feel him – all of him. His long legs, his large feet, his toes.

I wanted one last time to know him, feel him, touch him, kiss him, love him.

My guy. My strong, sexy guy. My Rodg.

I crawled into bed and held him to me all afternoon. I knew the end would come and I wanted, needed, to have him die in my arms.

I wouldn't let go. I held him, talked to him, prayed for him.

Told him it was time to fly away.

He would not do this alone. We were together always – my husband, my lover, my best friend, my partner, my travel buddy.

He would not make this last trip alone.

He was calm for hours and then began breathing heavily, shakily. No agitation, just labored breathing as his body shut down.

A final morphine push.

A pause.

A sigh.

An end to an amazing life.

10:37 p.m.

May 31, 2009.

Rodger died exactly one week after his first stroke. A week where we descended into Dante's seven layers of hell.

But now, it is finished.

Those were reported to be Jesus' last words. I feel they should be mine.

This weeklong nightmare is over. You did die in my arms – as I wanted and needed.

Was it peaceful? At the end, yes.

Oh my love, I hope I did right by you. I have to believe you were already gone on Wednesday. If you felt any pain I would kill myself.

Wait for me.

Someday I'll join you but for now I need to take care of our Boo - your strong little girl. She went home yesterday. I didn't want her to stay and see the end. Know that her last memory of her Daddy is a calm, peaceful one. You just looked like you were sleeping.

No evidence of a stroke.

No drooping mouth.

No tubes.

Just Rodger.

I would not have made it through the week in one piece with my sanity intact if it weren't for my family. All the kids came and stayed until I sent them home to rest.

Stephen blew off work and was with me 24/7. He was my advocate with Rodger's doctors and could explain everything to me. He negotiated with the nurses for better care, made me rest and kept me calm in the middle of the storm.

Tricia handled the hundreds of phone calls from friends, clients, the community. She was the information hotline and kept them all away so I could concentrate on Rodg. She brought me food and made sure I ate. She brought in clothes, and spelled me so I could take a walk, a breather, a pause.

I sent my brother John, who is hospital phobic, home with my mom. He kept her busy the whole week and kept her calm. She wanted to be a part of it. Wanted to help. But I could only handle so much. Steve, Trish and I had a rhythm, a team in place.

With their support I was able to stand, and was able to stand it.

Was able to make the decisions, make the calls, the DNR order. They held me together, and held me up at the end.

Just seconds after Rodger had passed, Dr. Doom, the really horrible doctor as we'd nicknamed her, came barreling in. I've never seen Tricia act so fast. She literally lifted the woman up by the elbows and propelled her out of the room, saying, "My sister needs more time."

And that was their mantra all week – what their sister needed. And they gave it to me.

Nothing is certain but death and taxes, and I think there is about as much paperwork with death.

God bless my sister. She was with me the last few days, and we talked about arrangements. Rodg wanted to be cremated - that was certain. So on Sunday, I kind of flipped out and sent Trish on a mission.

I'd heard horror stories about being overcharged for a cardboard box to hold the ashes. Why I was worried about that on this day, I don't know, but it distracted me.

So I sent her on an "urn run."

Find me a container for the ashes.

Somehow I thought the whole cremation thing would be over in a day or so and we'd need a box. I hadn't counted on the state of California. It takes longer to cremate someone than bury them. Almost two weeks longer, actually.

But how was I to know?

So she left at noon. Now this is a woman who, as a costumer, shops for a living. She can find a banana costume for a five year old. I knew she'd come through.

But she was gone a long time.

When she returned at 5 p.m. I asked what took so long.

She had a variety of options for me. Ginger jars, bread boxes, Parisian themed containers. Wooden cases. Everything you could think of.

Plus a car full of patio cushions.

Seems that while she was shopping she ran into a sale.

It was a much-needed laugh on a serious day, and we ended up using the cushions at my house for the memorial - they looked better than our tired old ones.

I chose a beautiful wood grained box that didn't look funereal. It looked like a gentleman's dresser case. Perfect.

One more detail down.

One more decision made in the bizarre alternate reality I was living.

It was pretty. It was practical. It was a decision that was easy to make.

The others weren't as easy.

Dealing with the mortuary was brutal.

It was final.

And as nice as they were, it was macabre.

First, there are a lot of distracting options on the shelves. I was glad we'd gotten a tasteful, elegant box all on our own.

You name it, you can be buried in it.

Faux golf bags. urns with Jesus, the Virgin Mary or the Virgin of Guadalupe on them. Footballs. Mugs. Southwest themed jars. Mini boxes in case the family wanted to divvy their loved one up.

Share the joy.

I was still in shock. The paperwork kept coming and I kept signing. I really counted on Trish to keep it straight. I thought we'd authorize it and be done with it. Rodg could be cremated in a day or two and

I could bring him home. I could leave Palm Springs and never come back.

Not so fast. bucko.

The state requires reams of paperwork, approvals, authorizations and signatures. You can get buried in a day (ask any Jewish friend) but you can't get cremated in less than a week. There's no rational, it's just bureaucratic b.s. designed to make the grieving process even more traumatic and drawn out.

The only thing I wanted was to have Rodger cremated in the summer travel coat he wore to Big Bear and his Fresno State hat.

I fixated on that and could give a shit about anything else.

For me it was already over.

But they kept sliding papers in front of me to sign. Trish kept track, and kept me on track. And at the end she shepherded me to the car and drove me back to L.A.

I was finished.

I was numb.

I'd left my baby in the hands of these strangers, and had to have faith they would treat him well.

It was the longest ride of my life, leaving him. I only prayed they would put him in his coat and hat.

We got home and I carried the empty box to our bedroom and put it on the dresser. It would be weeks before we could make the trip back.

There was no finality.

He was gone, but there was no body, no resting place, no ashes.

It was an ignominious non-ending.

Two weeks of waiting, of imagining what was being done to him, of not having closure.

So in the end it was I, not Rodger, who was in limbo.

After Rodger and I said I do, he never did.

Take off his wedding ring, that is.

For twenty-two years he never took it off. It was the only piece of jewelry he wore, other than a watch.

My guy's guy. No bracelets, chains or other baubles.

Just a plain gold band he wore day and night.

In the hospital he got so thin that it slipped off while we were doing his handprints.

I put in on my right ring finger to save it.

And since that day, I've never taken it off.

A week already.

Sunday night at 10:30 was the worst. Going to bed without you is unbearable. I can fake it at work; I am so busy with people coming in crying to me. I can comfort them because my heart is already broken.

Oh my love, I don't know if I can do thirty years of this.

Every picture, every pillow, everything reminds me of you. Somehow the office is okay, but home is so tough. I'm trying to keep it on even keel for Kate – this is such an important time in her life – graduation, freedom, new job. She is excited about working at Nordstrom, her friends, her college plans. I don't want to always be the miserable mom.

I cry myself to sleep but let her be a happy girl. She misses you horribly, but like all kids that age is resilient. She is certainly more loving, caring, affectionate. She is trying to take care of me.

We're two wounded birds trying to keep our nest together.

Rodger was a newspaper man his whole life.

What better way to pay him tribute than in the paper?

He had won the Chamber's highest award the year before. I had written his bio for that, so writing the obituary wasn't as brutal as it could be.

It was still written through a flood of tears.

I placed it with the *L.A. Times* - what a rip! I knew they charged - but $2000 for an obit with picture? Please, they are just preying on the grieving at that point.

But he was so important to the community it had to be done.

In our own papers he was the front page.

I had a great picture of him holding stacks of our newspapers. He's smiling, he's happy, he's Rodg.

I sent out emails to everyone I knew asking for them to send back a few words about him. The tributes filled up pages of the paper, and were amazing. People loved my guy. They respected him, laughed with his column, missed him already.

They ranged from professional nods to personal recollections. Colleagues and friends flooded my email with their accolades, and I put them all in the paper.

This was his town, his newspaper, and his memory.

I have known men who were intelligent in the ways that count. I have known men who could bring out a laugh so deep and real it was as if it was drawn up from the heart. I have known men who built businesses from the ground up, and men who left their mark in much more important ways on those who crossed their paths. But I have never known all of that and so much more in one man, until Rodger gave me the honor of calling him my friend. The first time I met Rodger was at his birthday party. There must have been 100 people celebrating his day, of whom I knew exactly two. But when I walked in with my wife, Rodger made sure to sit us at his table, and then spent the evening making us feel -- as was his way of making everyone feel -- as though we were the only ones in the room. As though we were his guests of honor. Rodger lived his life with courage, hope, and the strength to laugh even, and maybe especially, in the toughest of times. He honored me by his friendship. It is now up to me and all of his friends to earn that honor everyday of our lives by being the person he was, and passing on the gifts he gave us to those whose paths we may cross.
Steve Tully

Rodger Sterling was my next-door neighbor. When we moved in seven years ago, before he even knew our names he invited us over for a welcoming glass of wine. That glass turned into several bottles, and when we finally stood up to leave, bellies sore from laughing, we introduced ourselves, staggered home, and a truly great friendship blossomed from there. With his beautiful, generous, caring wife and stunning, brilliant daughter, I have always felt like I have family 100 feet away. His quick wit, insight, stories, love of all things automotive,

national pride and community involvement is truly inspirational to me. I don't know how old that handsome, rugged man was, but whatever the age, he left us far too soon.
God bless his shining soul.
Paul & Juli Scrivano

Rodger, Rodger, Rodger, what a warm, loving man. I loved Rodger because he gave so much love to everyone, but most of all it was how much he loved Kathleen. When he'd mention her name and where they were going on this trip or that, you could hear the love in his voice. Rodger, I will miss you.
Deborah Peters

"Rodger Sterling made us laugh. Behind the smile and the joke was a serious man who worked hard and long at his profession. He was a newspaperman, a family man and a builder of the community. His spirit is in every tree and every building and every street in the Valley... His death is our loss."
Don X Sanelli

Several years ago I invited Rodger and Kathleen for an impromptu dinner at our house, saying, "Just come as you are." About an hour later the doorbell rang and lo and behold there was Rodger all dressed up in a dress, high heels and a hat! Of course I was laughing hysterically and Rodger said, "Well you said, "Come as you are!"
Jerry and Patty Humes

" As a charter member of The Weird Humor Club, I mourn the loss of one of our major contributors. I hope his warm smile is well received wherever he is, and that his sense of humor lives on. I forgive him the lousy jokes he sometimes attributed to me, and the rumor that a compendium of his jokes will be submitted for Pulitzer Prize consideration is unfounded. Rodger, we - and our community - miss you."

Sy and Gloria Feerst

Los Angeles Times Obituary. June 6, 2009

Rodger Sterling, Editor and Publisher of *Valley News Group*, died peacefully May 31 after suffering a stroke.

Sterling was a second- generation newspaperman, having started as a teenager with the *Sanger Herald* outside of Fresno where his father was publisher.

He spent time in Detroit as an advertising executive (the first real "Roger Sterling" of the Mad Men television series!) where his clients included Lee Iacocca and John DeLorean.

Sterling bought the *Las Virgenes Enterprise* in Calabasas in 1968 from Alice Stelle, who had founded the paper to bring water and schools to the Las Virgenes community. He expanded the weekly paper from just Calabasas to include Agoura and Westlake Village.

Sterling was president of the Calabasas Chamber in both 1970 and 1974. During his tenure at the Chamber he started the Calabasas Pumpkin Festival in 1971.

Always involved in the community, Sterling was known for his warmth, his sense of humor, his love for his family and amazing recap of news and history, of both the community and World War II, which was his passion. He personally knew many of the pioneers of the area, and was a chronicler of the history and growth of Calabasas.

He was famous for his down-home "Fresno" sense, and the way he treated everyone with openness and warmth, regardless of their position. He had coffee for 25 years with the same group of friends at Howard Johnson's, now Red Robin.

He also met Richard Nixon in his father's kitchen in the 50's when Nixon was a senator, rode horses at Ronald Reagan's Malibou Lake Ranch and "put his dogs up" with President Gerald Ford when Ford visited Warner Center.

In 1985 he met Kathleen Bercsi, who owned the *Warner Center News*. They married and subsequently purchased the *Valley Vantage*. They ran the three papers together and always focused on what Sterling called "what's in it for the reader journalism." His favorite quote was "lousy local is better than wonderful wire" and he dedicated his career to bringing all local news to his readers.

He wrote his "English Channel" column of jokes, anecdotes and insights for over 50 years.

Sterling was President of California Newspaper Publisher's Association Southern California branch, and past president of the Valley Press Club. He was also had served as an active and vocal board member of the Woodland Hills Chamber of Commerce.

He also at different times owned the *Carpenteria Herald*, the *Agoura Valley News* and the *Woodland Hills Enterprise*, and was instrumental in starting the *Malibu Surfside News* and the *Marina del Rey Argonaut*.

He is survived by his wife Kathleen, and his children – Victoria, Katie, Bruce (Bobbi Jo), Marc (Nicole) Doug (Michelle) grandchildren Alexis and Shayla and his brother Ronald G. Sterling.

In lieu of flowers the family is requesting donations be made to the Rodger Sterling Journalism Scholarship at Fresno State.

Memorial services will be private.

I don't go to psychics.

I don't even read my horoscope.

But I see gold Cadillacs.

Doesn't pack quite the same punch as "I see dead people," but true nonetheless.

It started the day after Rodger died. Barely coherent, I was driving to the bank when I just lost it. Crying for Rodg, I told him I didn't know if I could do it. If I could go on with the business of newspapers - and of life - without him.

I needed a sign.

I needed to know somehow that he was still with me, that I hadn't lost him completely. I had no idea what I was asking for. I just knew that his death had been too sudden, too shocking, too fast for me to grasp it all. I had lost him, but couldn't face it.

Stopped at a red light, hunched over the steering wheel, I sobbed. "I need to know you're okay. I need to know you haven't left me entirely."

I didn't really know what I needed.

I just knew I wasn't ready to face his death and face reality.

Up next to me pulled a gold Cadillac, just like Rodger left in the driveway at home. I managed to laugh through my tears and say, "Okay, maybe that's my sign," and go on as the light changed.

I turned the corner and pulled up to the next light. As that light changed, another different make and model, but still gold, Cadillac flew by me.

Now I really got it.

That was his sign, my crazy car guy. He was letting me know he heard me. Hadn't flown far. Was still looking after me. Driving close by.

It made me feel better. It was weird, I'll admit, but it really made me feel he wasn't so far away. Maybe I hadn't lost him completely. Maybe we were still connected.

I'm pretty well grounded.

But I'd never lost a husband before.

I'd never been so alone.

I'd never been looking for any kind of message.

But there it was. A gold Cadillac in my rear view mirror, just when I was missing him, needing him, talking to him.

And I've seen one every day since.

Katie graduated a week after Rodger died.

I don't remember much about that week, but do know I made it clear to everyone that I wanted this day to be all about her. We would deal with the memorial after.

The Baccalaureate Mass was held Friday night. At first I thought to go in late, and duck out early to avoid everyone. But then I realized it was a good time to get a lot of the condolences out of the way. I knew I'd be seeing all the same people the next day, so if I went early friends could deal with the issue that night.

They prayed for Rodger at the mass and I lost it then, silent tears pouring down my face. But my girl and I made it through, holding hands through most of the service.

Graduation was beautiful. The high school does it formally, and when Katie came up the walk in her long white dress and gloves, holding a bouquet of roses, I was a proud mother.

I was also drugged.

My sister gave me a half of Xanax to get through it all.

Thank God, as we were seated in the front row. I held it together, though I could hear some of our friends crying when Kate walked by.

We had forty people to the house afterwards. All the family, good friends and a lot of Katie's buddies. I had admonished everyone that there should be "no tears today," and between the gifts, signing her picture board and feeding everyone, we did manage to make it a celebration.

I finally crashed about midnight. I drifted off to sleep hearing Katie and her friends talking outside at the bar. She really doesn't drink, but I thought if there ever was a time she might need one, it was now.

My little girl grew up a lot in that week.

Kate had so loved her father, and he was crazy about her. He said that it was easier to parent the second time around because he had more time, more wisdom and less fear.

Senior year all the girls had gone on retreat, a time of reflection as they left high school. A time for prayer, sharing and introspection. Each parent was asked to write their daughter a letter.

Rodger wrote his without my help. It was so beautiful, with all the things that were important to him about his girl. It brings me to tears to read it now, because he never got to live the last entries. He never got to see her graduate, leave for college, start her new life.

But it's filled with love, and beautiful memories. Reading it is reading a chronicle of our lives.

My guy. My girl.

It was a love letter to his daughter.

He created his own scrapbook for Katie. It was one of the last things he ever wrote, and one of the best.

Dear Katie:

Imagine a big blank scrapbook sitting in front of you. Let's call the book "our scrapbook" and let me fill it in with word pictures for you to remember our special times together.

*Turning to **Page 1**, I am immediately reminded of loving you while you were in the womb. Mom used to play opera so you would be cultured when you arrived. When she was out of site, I'd play cowboy music and you must have square danced in the womb because you started kicking. A little Fresno in a girl can't be all bad!*

***Page 2** -- We would surely display your youthful travel itineraries and travel regalia. I don't even think you were one year old when we hauled you along on our first trip to London. It was funny to see us go because you had twice or three times as much luggage as your mom and dad. We packed diapers, baby food and massive amounts of clothing and toys to keep you clean and warm. You were a great traveler too! And on one of our trips to London you received a gift from the plane of a drag-along suitcase. Boy, did you peacock pulling that "adult" luggage.*

***Page 3**-- We'd have to paste pictures of your first encounters with schooling and Ms. Casey. Remember your show biz debut in your flowery white tutu? And who was that glory-hound who kept trying to push you off the stage? Also memorable for me was your summer job with real money paid for real effort. Casey said you were one of the best student-teachers she had ever worked with. We were so proud.*

***Page 4**--Now we have pictures of you growing at St. Mel's. Years of Halloween Festivals? Or, how about a picture of us staring at the stars from that big telescope somebody loaned us for the night? Look, here's a picture of me waiting in that big old black Cadillac to bus you home while you told me about your day.*

***Page 5**--At the home front I remember us planting spring flowers together. Or, how about a photo of you and Boots racing from the back of our backyard to the back door? You used to beat him every time-- today, not so much! Remember us planting that huge Xmas Tree near the driveway in the front yard. I never thought that tree would live beyond New Years.*

Page 6--Here we have photos of you entering school, getting acquainted with new friends and buying all the books and clothing you need for Louisville in "the company store."

On the flip side of this page, I mostly remember your tennis triumphs and how you grew to the point where you were first string varsity. I've slipped in a picture of me playing tennis at Agoura High just in case anyone was scouting you (or me!). Thank goodness you are moving on to college--I honestly don't know where we would put all the future honors and awards you would have won (unless we put them in the garage).

Page 7--This page should certainly show your activities in the student body elections along with you freedom to drive and range out to new adventures with your friends. Also, a picture of your mom worried about getting you into college. As if she didn't know you were a lead pipe cinch. I remember our dances together when gathered at the gym and boogie danced--I felt so badly because I don't like dancing much (ask mom) but I loved being with you as "Bond...James Bond! or a raggedy tag cowboy. You of course, looked great in your costumes. I'm adding a picture on this page of you in your old Irish green kindergarten costume in case you're desperate to crash the dance next year.

Page 8--I have filled this page with some of your buddies and some of your joint activities. For instance, what about the night you took them all ice skating? Or the famous scavenger hunt? And, gads, without you and your buds, how would that Japanese restaurant in Agoura succeed without your regular attendance with Sami, KJ, and the group?

Page 9--I promise to fill out these pages with your graduation activities when the time comes--a shot of you throwing your grad cap up in the air when you are finished with Louisville. Also, a picture of you getting in the plane off to Italy even though it comes before you graduate (pressures on now to graduate).

And 10--This page will remain blank for the time being but I figure it'll fill up quickly as we enroll you into college, find suitable living arrangements, photo some of your new friends and begin your old new life as a collegian.

I should care about healthcare, the tsunami in Asia, flooding in the fire zones.

But I've already been run over by the tsunami.

Burned by the fire.

Flooded out.

The worst has happened to me, so the news is anti-climactic.

The bottom of *my* world fell out, so what happens out in the real world is just news.

I went from being a news junkie to being indifferent.

I still scan two daily papers, watch the late news, listen to the radio.

But other than the random high-speed chase, it just isn't that compelling. Doesn't grab me. Rolls right over me.

I'm numb.

I wonder when I'm going to give a damn. When I'm going to feel again. When I will care about anything again.

I drove alone to Palm Springs to pick up the ashes.

Rodger.

My duty, my baby, my love.

This was my final gift to him.

Friends, family, all offered to make the two-hour drive. They thought it would be too much for me - rightfully so.

I was hysterical the whole way there. It's a major truck route, and I made sure to stay behind a sixteen-wheeler all the way. If I crashed into one, I wouldn't kill anybody but myself.

And from where I was coming from, from that was definitely an option.

I was going to pick up what remained of a man I'd lived with, and loved, for twenty-five years. Who had been so vital, so alive, and now was dead.

Burned and boxed.

Reduced to a bag of ashes.

But it was still Rodger, and I was bringing him home.

I'd always promised Rodger I wouldn't keep him in the dining room.

Our friend Ralph died at seventy-five, and his widow kept the box with his ashes on the sideboard. Whenever we were at the house we'd tap the box and talk to him. Rodg thought it was bizarre. I thought it was sentimental. I thought Ralph would like it, keeping up with all the news.

Rodger never saw the sense in taking up good land that could go to farming.

"Wrap me in two paper bags and bury me out back."

I agree with him. I don't visit graves. First off, I can't ever find where my father and grandmother are buried - in "Oakwood" - by the big oak.

The place is nothing *but* big oaks.

So I end up feeling guilty and sad and frustrated and pissed off, which isn't the intent when you go to pay respects. Secondly, I'm claustrophobic and can't envision being underground for eternity.

So Rodger's ashes are with me.

With a lock of his hair I cut at the hospital, the DVD from the memorial, a copy of my memorial speech, and little things that remind me of him, all in the wooden box.

Ashes are weird.

There's no other word for it. I grew up all my life hearing "dust to dust, ashes to ashes." But they aren't dust. They're more like gravel, and heavy as dirt. I hate to be the one to break it to you, but ashes aren't smooth and lovely; they're sort of rough and filled with big pieces of what must be bone.

Not for the squeamish.

But it's Rodg

I can touch the box every day. Talk to him. Next to it I have an amazing picture from the kids' wedding of us sharing a kiss. That picture watches over him, along with a photo of Kate as a baby. I keep the tall vase we bought (okay, I bought and he carried) in Prague, filled with flowers next to it. Not many people know he's there. That's okay.

It's my guy. Right there with me.

Three people asked me to plan their funerals after Rodger's memorial. One thing I can do in my sleep is plan a party.

Having something to do probably kept me sane the first weeks after he died. I would go to work, deal with the paper and go straight into party planning mode.

This was the only thing the kids and I disagreed on. Two of them wanted the big hoopla at his favorite restaurant, open to the public. They argued that he was such a prominent member of the community that the community should share in his service.

I put my foot down.

I did not want a chamber mixer, an open party, a cluster fuck.

I wanted it to be personal, and private, and only for those who knew and loved him. I'd been at too many of those services, where people showed up for free drinks and gossip.

I made it clear it was invitation only. I sent out cards with a picture of Rodger in his travel coat and hat, taken just the month before in Venice, inviting them to the house for a memorial and dinner following.

Kate and I pulled every album, every bin of photos, out of the garage and sorted through them. I'm the family photog - so we must have gone through over a thousand pictures.

A thousand memories.

A thousand tears.

We cried a lot. Laughed. Looked at everything from his parents' photo album to her baby pictures. Our trips, our parties, our life together.

A wonderful, painful, joyful, emotional bonding experience.

I picked out music to go with each section - from "Come Fly With Me" for our first days together to "Girl from Ipanema" for our trip to Costa Rica. The kids got "You Are the Sunshine of My Life," and Katie's pics were accompanied by "Isn't She Lovely?" I ended the video with a picture of Rodg with all our friends and the song "Smile." I haven't been able to put on a Sinatra CD since. Too much.

The video got made.

The food ordered.

The booze stacked on the patio.

I counted two hundred of our nearest and dearest and planned for that.

I agonized over centerpieces until a friend had a brilliant idea. We took the antique typewriters from the office and placed one on each table. So fitting. So Rodger.

I didn't want a religious service. We really didn't go to church. He loved watching Robert Schuller on television Sunday morning. "My church service," he called it. I was hit or miss at mass.

Our friend Steve had sent the paper the most beautiful, fitting tribute, so I had him start with a eulogy. We followed with a Hebrew prayer for the dead.

Then the killer.

For my war historian, inspiration hit at 3 a.m. I hired the Confederate Air Force to do a flyover of the house.

They came up from the beach and over the mountain at the appointed time. You could hear the old World War II trainers as they lumbered up the canyon. I had everyone look east as the planes appeared. They swooped low over the house and circled back over the mountain.

Then they returned.

As they flew over the yard they headed towards the sky and performed the missing man formation.

One plane blew smoke, separated from the others, flying off solo.

Tears rolled down every upturned face.

My wounded bird had flown away from us, and the symbolism of the missing man was immortalized in a photo that hangs on our travel wall.

Rodger's last trip.

Once again I told him to fly away, and we all said goodbye.

With friends and family, we sent my guy home.

At the memorial service my daughter-in-law asked me if the rumor was true.

"Rumor?"

"That Rodger died during sex."

Oh God. He'd love that.

It was a light moment in an otherwise somber day. I guess the story came about from the headboard banging.

His kids thought he'd died during sex.

"No. He didn't pull an Alfred Bloomingdale," I told her. "He didn't die in the saddle."

But we had a good laugh, and I loved the thought.

"You certainly did it enough."

I raised my eyebrows and told her that the night before had been quite a ride, but no, it wasn't true. I don't think I could have handled that.

But out of such rumors come legends, and Rodg was now one notch up with his boys.

It's a grand old flag.

But what do I do with it?

At the mortuary they asked if Rodger was a veteran, or had been in the armed services.

Now Rodger didn't exactly see combat in the Air National Guard. He loaded bombs into planes that I guess flew around California pretending to look busy.

This was in the late 50's. Post WWII and Korea, and before Vietnam. I'm not sure if it was compulsory, or he signed up for it. All I know is he said he spent six long months dodging bullets on former farm land and learning to shine his shoes.

Evidently that's close enough for government work.

When I picked up his ashes they gave me a small box with a flag in it.

Lovely.

Rodg actually hated his time at the National Guard, but I grew up with a brother in the military and a staunch American father.

So you don't just toss it in the back of the closet.

I thought it would be a nice touch at the memorial, so the day of the service I pulled it out of the box.

There must be professional flag folders hidden somewhere in a secret lab. The box was only twelve by twelve inches, but the flag that emerged from it was eight feet by ten feet.

This thing could fly over the White House.

One more detail on a day of crushing details and decisions.

We hung the flag on the back of the gazebo as a backdrop. My sister steamed out the wrinkles - there were tons as the thing was origamied into the box.

It was a nice touch. No one really commented on the flag itself being there, but they did on the size. It also served to keep the sun off the front row seats.

I could have lied and said Rodger had a distinguished military career. His government was honoring him for service to God and country. But I couldn't pull it off, and neither could he.

Rodg was in no way military material. He was too loose, too lax and too irreverent. He did his duty, albeit grudgingly, without valor or victory. But his shoes weren't shined to perfection, and he never cut his hair regulation length. No one would buy it.

So I told the truth. It came out of the box and I put it up.

In reality, I was stuck with the damn thing. It was a nice footnote to the day, and added to the solemnity of the occasion. But it was one more thing to worry about.

When it was time to take it down, it was Katie who actually folded it into a neat triangle, all tucked and cornered and perfect.

"Where did you learn that?" I asked my teenage daughter.

"In first grade."

I think she might follow in her father's illustrious footsteps.

I'm trying not to second-guess God.

Trying not to look back to see if I could have changed the outcome.

I could have put Rodg on a low fat, low cholesterol diet. Could have gotten a carotid artery scan. Could not have taken him to Big Bear. Could not have had sex at that altitude. Could not have taken him for the invasive bladder check up.

Should have could have would have - what?

I married a meat and potatoes guy. He loved his steak, red wine. He had pie for breakfast on vacation. He was who he was. He carried a bum heart and his time was up.

In the hospital I'd pointed out his earlobes to Steve. Large and floppy - some studies indicate that's a sign of heart disease later in life. Who knows?

Later is now.

The heart disease caught up with him. Could I have prevented it?

I'm not a doctor.

I'm not God.

I'm just a wife who can't look back and say if I'd done this or that the stroke wouldn't have killed him.

If I look back it will kill me.

❧

I cry in the car.

It's safe there, and it's usually the only time during the day I'm alone.

I haven't broken down at the office yet, but in the car I can talk to Rodg and play music that reminds me of him.

It's when I see the Cadillacs.

They're there when I need them. When I'm talking to him, crying over him, missing him, needing a sign. I've seen one every day.

He's still with me.

He's still speaking straight to my heart - without saying a word.

Joni Mitchell sang "Leave 'em laughing when you go."

I feel that's how I've been the last couple of months. I haven't shown the grieving widow face to the world. I haven't wanted to bum people out. But I am still grieving from the bottom of my toes to the top of my aching head.

Alone, I don't have to pretend.

Don't have to entertain.

Don't have to be "on."

Don't have to fake it.

I can just be me. I can cry when I need to. I can also reflect on the story of us.

God, we were lucky.

We were so in love. Shared so much love.

Did everything together for twenty-five years. People always ask me how we could be together 24/7 for that long. It's because we were partners, lovers, best friends. I hesitate to use the words "soul mate," but from the moment we met we were joined together. He was the up to my down, the smile to my frown, my cheerleader with all my activities, the balm that eased my crazy angst, the person that completed me in every sense of the word.

I was his refuge, his strength, his biggest fan, his buddy, his "all American girl."

We talked day and night, and sometimes didn't need to talk at all. He would smile at me across a room, and lift his eyebrows to ask if I was all right. We let our bodies show how much we loved each other all night. He knew.

He lived knowing, and he died knowing.

I knew too. That's why it hurts so much now. It's this big gaping hole in my heart. I keep looking over my left shoulder for him. He was always there. He was always riding "drag" to cover my back.

Now that he's gone I'm only half of what we were together.

But only I know that.

I've been seeing a grief counselor, well, for a while.

Even before Rodger died I saw him to deal with the fallout of my dad's death. I loved my father, but had a lot of unresolved issues and Mark helped me through them.

With Rodger, he probably saved my life.

I called him from the hospital after the second stroke. I remember sitting on the floor outside the hospital room, sobbing and telling him that Rodger was dying.

He talked me down and talked me through it.

I saw him every week for months. Only there could I let down. Only there could I be honest about how I didn't think I could make it. In that room I didn't have to be strong. I didn't have to keep it together for Katie. I didn't have to pretend to be okay.

He told me what I was feeling was normal. Was part of the grief process. He walked me through exercises and had me write a letter saying goodbye to Rodger.

Brutal.

Tough.

Painful.

The theory was that writing a letter would help me realize he was gone. Physically, not emotionally. I'd never lose the connection but had to lose the notion that it was all a dream.

None of it was easy, some of it was impossible, but week after week I gradually felt that I was getting better. Moving forward. Learning to live with the pain.

When I finally got through talking about the night of the stroke and Rodger's death, I told him about the gold Cadillacs. He listened to me, and said he couldn't comment on what I called the "woo woo" stuff, but if it made me feel better, go ahead and believe it.

He and Katie both think I rely too much on seeing a car every day, and that one day I'm going to lose it if I don't.

Whether they are real or imagined, the do give me comfort. I believe it. I need it, and I like thinking he's still with me.

One day I had something else to discuss with him. I only hoped he'd still keep me on as a client.

When the fog of the hospital and the memorial finally cleared, I awoke one morning bitchy, itchy and horny, aching for a man who wasn't there.

Ready to climb the walls, wound as tight as a coiled spring, and just as volatile.

From a daily habit to quitting cold turkey.

Sixty to zero in no time flat.

From a regular, healthy sex life to none at all.

When I realized what had gotten under my skin - or not gotten under as the case may be, I thought it through. So randy you could bend me over and fuck me till Sunday - but that wasn't an option.

I didn't want sex with just any man.

I wanted sex with my husband.

There was the maybe, the possibly, the probability of having sex with someone else, but just that. I couldn't imagine sharing intimacy, talking all night with someone, taking someone else in my mouth - my prurient fantasies stopped at that.

Couldn't go there.

To me, oral sex is something so intimate. Unlike the current crop of teens or the former President, to me that is one of the most giving of acts - to have his mouth on me or mine on him.

So I wasn't running out to the nearest bar.

Wasn't looking around for the next possible candidate.

I wanted Rodg, but he wasn't here.

So it was up to me. It wasn't that I wasn't used to touching myself-we had tried every variation, every position, everything we wanted to do - together. I certainly had no problems when he was around.

But my first attempt to get myself off was an abysmal failure.

It took too long and was too boring. Not exactly enough to get me to peak. I cried through the entire process at the emptiness of the act, the loss of consortium, the missing him from the depth of my soul.

My bed mate.

My sex partner.

My ardent lover.

I didn't know what to do next. Not only did I have to face a life without him, run a business without him, raise a teenager without him - I had to figure out how to have sex without him.

I brought the issue to therapy. Mark never knew what to make of me anyway, and I opened with "you're going to love today." Sometimes I laugh as much as I cry in there. I can be open and honest with him. It's not just that I'm paying him to listen to my rambles, cries and complaints, but he really gets me and my issues.

So he listens as I stumble around the word masturbation.

It's easier for me to use dirty words than to cough that one out. I tell him if I just wanted to get laid I could probably find a candidate or two - even at my current weight – but that wasn't what I wanted. I just wanted to stop climbing the damn walls in frustration.

He told me I didn't have to lose Rodger in bed.

I didn't have to lose that intimacy with him.

Mark told me next time I tried to make myself come to put Rodger in my head. To remember what he did, and said, and how he touched me. Remember how good it was, and how it felt. How he felt, and how I felt, when his hands, his mouth were on me.

To basically bring Rodger back to bed with me.

So I did. I actually made a "date" with him in my head. I thought about it all day, and how I was going to do this. It's another one of those strange realities I never thought I'd experience. But I needed, wanted, desperately had to find some relief. I'm a normal, healthy, forty-nine year old woman with urges and desires. I miss my husband. I miss our intimacy.

I miss sex.

God, do I miss sex.

So round two. This time I took it slow. I put Rodg in my head and really listened. I heard him murmur to me. I heard him talk about the line of my neck, my white thighs, the soft curve of my breast, the crease where thigh meets hip. I heard him telling me what he's going to do. What he likes, how I taste, how I feel, and I'm able to take myself over and come with him.

It takes longer, it's not as much fun, and it's certainly not as complete. I miss his weight on me. I miss him in me.

The sweat, the smells, the primal act.

But in my mind I hear, I feel and I am able to finally find, if not total fulfillment, at least not total frustration.

Afterwards there are still tears. But they are tears of release and joy that I haven't lost the connection, the ability to feel, to remember, to be loved. Even now.

I lay spent in our bed and stare at the ceiling.

I hold the jacket to me, turn my face into it, and smile.

I could feel him on my hands.

Kate and I had decided to sprinkle some ashes at Rodger's favorites spots on our mother-daughter trip to Europe. At "our bench" under the Eiffel Tower. Rue Cler where we spent so many vacations. Leicester Square in London. The Sherlock Holmes Hotel bar where we had many a high tea.

So one night when she was out I took the heavy bag to the kitchen. I had washed and dried out a bubble bath bottle I had bought in London... fitting for his return. Also took a small baggie in case they tried to throw the bottle away at airport security.

I wasn't going to lose him again.

With a funnel and tears tried to transfer ashes. Not as easy as it sounds, so some spilled on the counter. I laughed through the sobs and said, "Welcome home." I couldn't bear to clean it up with a sponge - somehow sacrilegious - so with my fingers dusted up the excess.

Couldn't wash it off. Couldn't take that part of him and cavalierly wash him away.

I have to say it was comforting. I had a piece of him with me.

Flying out, I called my friend from the airport on the other side of the TSA screeners and let her know, "Rodger made it through security."

So he took one final trip.

Not everyone realizes I got hit with a double whammy.

Rodger died at the beginning of the summer, and at the end of it Kate left for college.

Freshman year.

Not only was I an "empty nester," but I had a completely empty nest. I was alone come September.

I returned from work every night to a quiet house. I avoided it as much as possible and cried every time I headed home. With only the cat to keep me company, I was miserable.

I have friends who told stories of sending their kids to college. One woman didn't get out of bed for three days. My best friend was so hysterical when her daughter left for school I didn't even recognize her voice when she called.

But I slowly learned how to be alone. How to be self-sufficient. Kept the CD player or the news on until I fell asleep. Did all the chores Rodg used to do. Felt satisfaction the first time I cleaned the fireplace. Changed the recessed lighting.

But when I crawled into bed it was just me. When I awoke it was just me. It was all I could do to drag myself out of bed and start another day.

I had to do something. I had to start something. Something I could actually look forward to.

In the hospital my daughter-in-law had given me a journal.

"Write it down. Let it out. You need a release," she told me, since I never left the room.

I just kept writing.

In September when Kate left, I talked to friends about what to do. I needed something.

Anything.

Something to occupy my time. Distract me. Challenge me. Several of them had played around with writing a book over the years, but were stalled.

So it was I the organizer, the person that can never sit still, that said, "Let's start a writing group. Let's force ourselves to meet ever week so we write every week." So we do.

It comes pouring out of me, usually at 4 a.m. Typing and tears in the middle of the night. But it's cathartic, and I love the group. We each bring something to read aloud, and then discuss it. We are baring our stories, and our souls to each other. A wonderful experience, even though I embarrass the guys sometimes.

But it's a sacred space, where we can read and open up and share that which is closest to us.

It makes my whole week.

I crave intimacy.

I long for touch.

Reaching out in the middle of the night to find him there. Being pulled into his arms, smelling his scent. Being stroked, petted, loved. The soft murmurs, the low laughter in the dark.

I miss running my hands over the body I know as well as my own. Playing with his chest hair, putting my hands on his face. It's not always sexual, but a knowing, wonderment that yes, he belongs to me, and I to him.

I could wrap myself around that reassurance.

Rodger used to pull me to him and bury his face in my hair. He would whisper, "I love you so much" and just envelop me. It was love, it was security, it was everything I ever wanted or needed.

I was the last thing he reached for at night and the first thing he saw in the morning.

I was safe there. Burrowed into him I was protected, loved, beautiful. Our room, our bed, was really our sanctuary. No cash flow, no family drama, no stress, just the two of us at our most loving, our most elemental.

We could stay like that forever, holding on to each, drawing from each other, or we could drift into slow, easy lovemaking – a quiet sharing and coming together.

Now there is a void.

It is not just the empty side of the bed.

It is the hole in my heart.

The empty air I cannot grab onto.

There is nothing, and no one there to touch. The actual energy of lying beside a warm, breathing person is gone. It is the black hole of aloneness.

I remember seeing a TV special years ago on baby Rhesus monkeys. I watched in horror as they separated them from their mothers. They put half in cages with a live female, and the other half in cages with a robot. The infants with the mechanical, metal, unfeeling, unloving mother died within weeks.

I ache to be held.

What the hell do you do all day?

I sit outside on the patio and talk to you all the time.

I don't hear back.

I share everything I've done. What the work crises are. The latest on my mom. Kate and school. The gossip.

There's so much to tell you.

I know you listen. I know you hear.

But are you okay?

No one really can explain what goes on in the hereafter. But I need to know.

Are you out of pain? Happy? Floating free?

Do you see Dale, Dad, McCord, all the guys that went before you?

All the books on heaven can't answer that basic question.

I have to believe that you are now free from the physical constraints. That the stroke was over and done with here on earth. That you're in no pain. That you're happy and set free.

But I don't know.

So I keep talking to the stars and hoping they twinkle a little brighter when I'm done.

He's not coming back.

It's a punch to the gut.

I can go all day.

Running.

Pretending.

Avoiding.

Then it will hit me. The moment I stop - I remember.

And it hurts, just as much.

And so I wonder. What is all this for?

He's not coming back.

I'm busting my hump to keep the papers going, pay the mortgage, pay the bills. Why? Kate's college is paid for. The other kids are older and okay. I could always give them more. But they have their own lives.

It all seems so futile.

I'm a hamster on the wheel, running in circles because there's nothing else to do.

I'm not going to off myself, but I do ask, "What's the point?"

He's not coming back.

With all my work, all my lunches, all my friends - I'm still so alone.

I read that Queen Victoria - after Albert died - continued to have his clothes laid out every morning until she herself died more than forty years later. I know the feeling. I understand. Deep in your heart you want to believe. You want to believe he's not gone. You want to believe this is temporary. You want to believe that someday he will walk in the door.

That someday, he is coming back.

He's not coming back.

॰॰

I'm sure my neighbors think I'm the "Merry Widow."

I hated coming home alone. I had to do something to fight the loneliness.

So I made Thursdays a happening.

Over the summer after the paper was put to bed I'd invite a few friends over for "Thursdays in the Gazebo."

We'd sit outside, drink wine, have some cheese and crackers and just watch the week fade away.

Now they're something of an institution. I can have anywhere from five to twenty-five people show up. It's just an open house, open party. I never know who's coming, and that's what's great about it. It's friends, family, clients. I just send out a huge email and everyone who can come brings an appetizer or bottle of wine.

There are regulars. I keep milk in the fridge for one friend, who has to have it with dessert. Cigars for another. Imported beer for some. Candy for my six-year-old nephew. Good red wine for my friend Patty.

Sometimes we have theme nights. "Italian." "Mexican." "Tax Day Weenie Roast" where everyone brought receipts to burn and we roasted hot dogs in honor of those IRS weenies.

We've got a thing going. My chef friend TJ usually brings a main dish and sets up in the kitchen to cook. His wife quietly crochets, though last time she and I did an awful rendition of "Need You Now" using our cell phones as microphones. My brother brings his son and dessert. My mom brings Chardonnay and comes to hang out. She loves my friends and they adore her. One woman, no matter how much I protest, does dishes at the end of the night.

There are cars and people in and out all night. Music plays on the outside speakers. Sometimes we light a fire in the fire pit. The boys sit outside and smoke. Our semi-professional astronomer drags everyone outside to show us the night sky.

It's an event. It's fun and crazy and really good to get this group together. Restaurant owners have met other restaurant owners. We were the "test kitchen" for a friend's new place, and got toasted when he had us taste all the different choices for his house wine. People who'd never met before now talk about their week with friends they've made. It's loud music, lots of talk, lots of laughter.

The house is full of life again for a few hours.

❧

Today was the last day of Nascar season. Rodger would have been glued to the TV.

He loved cars and in our twenty-five years together must have bought over thirty cars. Some he never drove. They sat in the garage for years as "saver cars" – everything from a 70's Transam to a '37 Chrysler.

I used to joke that Rodg could just sit naked in the front seat, go "vroom vroom" and be perfectly happy. We always made money when we sold them so it was okay, except it was a bitch to get anything out of the garage when we needed it.

He'd talk cars endlessly with his sons, friends, everyone and anyone. I once caught him staring at a beautiful blond in a convertible. I kidded him about it and he turned a confused face to me. "What blond?" He was staring at the car.

When we first met I had season tickets to the Hollywood Bowl. Rodg took me to the Saugus Speedway. Way more exciting! I loved the noise, the action, the beer and the boys. Really dug the "train races," where they chained three cars together and raced in a figure eight until they crashed into each other. Total white trash, but crazy fun.

Rodger watched Nascar every Sunday. A Fresno boy at heart. He loved the American spirit of it all as much as the cars, and would tear up at the national anthem and the flyover. He loved that they still opened the race with a prayer.

He was proud to be a "merican" as he said, and not ashamed of it.

He was fast cars, apple pie and the American flag. He was a small town boy who never lost his small town values.

He never missed a race.

He never bought a foreign car.

Chest pain.

Shortness of breath.

Numb left arm.

BP 200 over 120.

Thought I was having a heart attack.

I ended up in the ER the week before Christmas. Got the world's most expensive check up in the hospital. Cardiac enzymes. EKG. Chest x-ray. Chem panel. All negative.

I'm the healthiest unhealthy person I know.

Combination of stress, hormones, too much caffeine, too much wine. My periods had stopped a year before Rodger's death, but after that they came back with a vengeance. I was trying hard to make a perfect Christmas for the kids, and worried about them falling apart.

Six months of self-indulgence and self-pity had caught up with me.

I was left with the diagnosis of a major panic attack and high blood pressure. Just great.

No more Diet Coke.

No more wine.

No salt.

Add that to no sex and there's not much to look forward to.

I'm a Diet Coke addict. My "breakfast of champions" was a huge soda from Jack in the Box. Client lunch with more DC. Dinner with two to three to four glasses of wine, depending on the night.

It numbed the pain.

It took the edge off.

It let me fall asleep without reliving the horror of the stroke, the week in the hospital, the last minutes of Rodger's life.

All the ghosts that haunt you in the middle of the night.

I was self medicating on legal uppers and downers.

And it took its toll.

So I faced the New Year clean, sober and unamped.

Because as much as I don't want to live, I don't want to die.

The high blood pressure freaked me out. Rodger died of a stroke, and I was terrified of the same fate. Or worse yet, a halfway job that left me a drooling vegetable.

So I cleaned up my act. The deprivation doesn't really bother me. I've lost so much it's just one more indignity piled on top of all the others.

I admit I sleep better. I spend a lot more time trying to get to sleep, but I'm not awake from 3 to 5 a.m. anymore with a sugar high.

But I miss the dull blade that cuts the hurt. I miss the numbness. I miss the creative juices let loose after a couple glasses of wine. I'm afraid I'm not as good a writer sober as I am when I've had a couple.

I'm afraid of the dark, and the memories that come with it.

I miss the shield of Chardonnay.

I'm losing weight and feeling guilty.

Several people told me I look better. The no soda, no booze diet is working

But it makes me sad. Rodger loved me the way I was. Extra weight and all. Now that he's gone I'm cleaning up my act and looking better. It's ironic. Of all people he should have benefited from a skinnier, healthier me. He loved me no matter what. He thought I was beautiful. He thought I was sexy.

And now that I'm getting thinner he's not around to enjoy it.

I do like the compliments. But the thought of turning into a different person bothers me in a way. I'm not ready to be attractive to someone else. I'm not ready to think about anyone else. I've never been a wallflower, but I'm not ready to think about dating.

I'm not sure I ever want to take on someone else's body, someone else's toenails, habits, sweats and smells. I don't know that I want to ever get that close to someone again.

I know losing weight isn't all about looking better. It's about being healthier for me. About being healthier to stick around and take care of Katie, my mom, my friends. About being there for the people that love me and need me.

But for years the weight has been a wall of defense. My mother called me a baby seal, the thin person I once was surrounded by a coating of fat. I don't know what I was protecting myself from, but Rodger loved me and that's all I needed.

I'm not going to stop the process. The blood pressure is dropping and I'm feeling better.

I just don't want to feel too much.

Losing the weight is like peeling layers off, exposing me, making me vulnerable. To what, I don't know.

I just know as much as I want it, want to look good again, it scares the hell out of me.

A big piece of plastic isn't going to replace him.

All my friends joke about buying me a vibrator. My single friends swear by them, and smile.

I can smile without one.

I'm sure it would be easier, and sure as hell faster, with a battery operated appendage.

It's just not me. I had no problem walking into those adult stores on the boulevard. I've bought party favors. I've bought gag gifts.

But I'm not ready to commit to the Erosolator. No lie, one friend said her *doctor* recommends this model.

I've got enough on my mind. Finding the perfect size and shape and color and speed just isn't on my agenda right now. I'm not saying no. I'm just saying not right now.

So far, my memories and me are doing fine.

But the jokes keep coming. I won't be surprised if I find one in my stocking this year. But it will probably stay sheathed (pardon the pun) for a while.

I'm not sure I'm ready for the Erosolater.

It's sort of like "Coke Zero." They can market it all they can.

It still doesn't replace "the real thing."

I'm making Christmas about the little ones. I have a bassinet filled with baby clothes from Paris. A pink retro 50's tricycle. Enough Limited Two shirts to outfit my granddaughter for the next year.

We're going to concentrate on the next generation. On new life.

We'll miss Rodg, and probably get through the gifts before we get into our cups and our tears.

But it will all be about family.

His family.

Our family.

My guys are coming home.

ॐ

"Today was a good day."

Rodg and I borrowed that phrase from Katie, who used to say it when she was little.

I cried a bit, especially when I knew she was going back to school after Christmas vacation.

But we got a lot done around the house. Got the tree outside, the lights down. Got on the treadmill for the first time in ages. Saw a movie with friends, then went to dinner afterwards.

I am home in bed, warm and content.

I still cry. I still mourn. But I'm learning to live on my own.

I have my own business. I have job security. I have a home I love, that I refinanced in the middle of this crisis. I paid off the credit cards. I have amazing friends. Both my brothers called me to wish for a new and better year. I'm seeing my sister tomorrow.

Best of all, Katie left me a note in the kitchen when she returned to campus. "Thanks for a great Christmas. Call me if you need anything. Love you mom!"

It doesn't get much better than that.

Hi Baby. Happy New Year.

I'm glad to see 2009 go - a roller coaster year from high to hell.

But I'm sad because it takes me even farther away from you. For so many it's the start of a new year. A new excitement. A new promise.

For me it's another step away from our life together. It's the closing of a chapter that was my whole life.

Life as part of a couple, a team, a family.

I can fake it pretty well. I hit a New Year's Eve party. Didn't know a lot of people but it was nice. Insanely good food. Good friends. Sweet because they asked me to text them when I got home so they knew I was safe off the freeway.

Went to another party where I just melted into my buddies. They get it. They know how hard this really is. They understand when I leave a New Year's party at 11 p.m. that I don't really need to ring in the New Year. I'm not in a mood to celebrate, or be festive. I love being with my friends, hearing their excitement about a new car, a son's college acceptance, a daughter's grades. We talk politics, laugh at jokes, listen to each other's stories. It's warm and familiar and I feel good being around them.

But at a certain point it's hard. I'm not part of a couple. I'm the solo act floating from group to group. I miss you. I miss looking "across a crowded room and somehow you'll know," having you scrunch your nose at me, our little sign of "Hi, honey, you doing okay?" I miss the ebb and flow of a couple, sharing laughter, sharing gossip on the way home, sharing memories of the old year and dreams for the new.

On the way home I shed my tears. I told you I wasn't ready for a new year. Not ready for a new life.

I want my old life.

The first half of 2009.

The life with you.

I listened to one of our favorite songs on the radio.

And through my tears I saw the gold Cadillac pull up in the fast lane and then pull ahead. And I felt your arms around me. I know you hear me. I know you're letting me know that from the other side you're still trying to give me what I need.

It's not enough.

But it's enough for tonight.

Some nights I'll have slept on the jacket, so when I pull it to me it's warm from body heat and I can pretend he's there.

I can pretend I'm holding him. Curved belly to back, my arms pulling him close.

We're entwined, my six-foot guy and me. My knees press the back of his and my thighs mold to him. We're two pieces of a puzzle that fit together.

I feel the warm jacket – and my body remembers.

છ

I'm recognizing my rhythm now. I can go forever on a project without losing it. If I'm working on getting out the paper, sending a big mailing to clients, or fixing up the house for the appraisal - I can go for hours focused on one thing.

I welcome the complete concentration. The all-absorbing work. The ability to think of nothing else.

And then the wake-up call.

I finish the project, the job, and reality bites. I'm alone again, and can think of nothing else.

This is why no one sees me break down. This is why everyone says I'm doing so well. They only see me coping. They don't see the drive home to the empty house. They don't see the hours from ten to midnight when no one calls, and no one answers in the silent rooms.

They don't see me, even six months later, curled up in a ball, crying my heart out.

Because I can focus. Always have. Always have been the perfect girl for everyone. The responsible one. The honor student. The oldest child.

It sucks living up to the image you've created.

For once I'd like to let loose and just have someone hold me. I'd like to cry on someone until there are no tears left.

I'm such a faker.

I am still so sad.

I am still so lost without him.

I am still so alone.

え

My car guy. My Nascar boy. My 'merican.

I keep seeing those gold Cadillacs. Some days only one when I need it.

Some days it's like a joke and I'll see several in an hour. I feel like he's teasing me - like he used to.

They turn up in the damndest places. And it's not like I'm seeing the same car over and over. They're all different. Different years. Different models. But all Cadillacs. And all gold.

I keep track. I don't want anyone to think I'm losing it. Or I'm a nutcase who talks to the little people only I can see.

The damn cars cut me off. Show up on the freeway when I'm crying. Show up only when I'm talking to Rodg.

One morning at Starbucks I was sitting my two of my closest friends, talking about Rodger and how much we had sex. No kidding. What else do you talk about at 8 a.m.? But it was a discussion about relationships, and someone brought up sex. My one friend said she was in awe of Rodger. At 70+ he was still doing it all the time - *without* Viagra.

She then turned to me and asked, "Did you see it? Did you see the gold Cadillac that just passed by?"

I could only laugh. I'm sure it was a big, old, struttin' one if he was following our conversation. I didn't see that one. But I'm glad someone else did.

We were talking about Rodger - and he heard it.

I miss morning sex. The melting together, the quiet rocking, the slow coming awake together, the slow come. Starting your day knowing you are so loved.

Fact is, I miss every kind of sex.

Make up sex. Romantic loving sex. The wild ride when you're half buzzed kind of sex. Just "get my rocks off" sex. "We've been married forever and know exactly what we like" sex. Try a new position and laugh sex.

Problem is, I miss it with Rodg.

So that limits my options.

He was the most generous of lovers. And so in love.

He would trace his hands over my face, rub his thumb over my mouth and kiss me before running his hands down my body.

He would lie atop me, his face turned at my neck, holding me, loving me, breathing me in.

He could be quiet and tender. He could be wild and raunchy. He could be every romantic dream, every fantasy.

And he was all mine.

During the day he was friends with everyone. He talked to everyone, was a citizen of the community, a publisher, a civic leader.

But in bed I had all his attention. All his love shining through. I came first, literally and figuratively.

It was incredible to have all that energy, all that love, intelligence, humor and creativity focused on me.

And I gave back. Anything and everything he wanted. Never said no. Never said no time. Never stopped loving him every way I could. We were partners in life, in love and in bed.

After twenty-five years we knew every inch of each other, every feel, every taste. It wasn't twice a day anymore, but it was twice as intense. We weren't young lovers, but we were seasoned lovers.

We didn't have to ask "Do you like this?" "Do you want this?" We just knew. And we reveled in it.

I miss it all.

෧ඁ

I always knew this day would come. I never took it for granted. What we had. How much we loved.

He was older.

It was always in the back of my mind, so every night I'd grab hold and hang on.

I'd pull Rodg to me and just breathe him in.

I think it's why we had such a beautiful sex life. We wanted to be as close as humanly possible, as much as possible. We loved each other, and the intimacy.

It's why we lived every moment to the max. Why we took so many trips. Getting on a plane and riding off into the sky with just the two of us, or the three of us with Katie, made it all worthwhile.

As I said in Rodger's eulogy - if we had two nickels to rub together, he'd say, "let's go!" And sometimes it was just that much. We stayed in some dive hotels in the first years together, but laughed and loved our way through them.

The London Continental - which sounds so much better than it was. The rooms were so small you could shower, brush your teeth and pee without moving an inch. The tiny room in France where the floor sloped south. Formula One on the way to Bruges where we slept in bunks and had to go down a sketchy hall to the toilet. The wonderful pension in Vienna with the winding staircase but miniscule hotel rooms and a common bath.

We upgraded rooms over the years, but never the memories.

I feel like I'm betraying him.

There are days when I actually feel kind of happy,

I saw the grief counselor and talked about the New Year. I'm feeling good some days - but feeling bad about feeling that way. Some days I go along for an hour or so and forget.

I'm feeling sad and guilty that I'm not more sad and guilty.

I'm doing so much and keeping so busy. I got the front doors refinished, the chimney cleaned after twenty-five years. Moved Kate's college fund into another investment. Started an IRA. Hired Joanne back at the office.

I feel like I'm accomplishing things and moving forward.

But I feel like I'm leaving Rodg behind. That I'm forgetting him.

Mark told me it was normal. That this is the next "phase" of this process. That I've put Rodger in his proper place. The reason that the highs and lows aren't roller coaster high or low anymore is that the shock has worn off. I've now put him into my memory bank. I haven't forgotten him - never can, never will, but now have realized that he's gone.

It made sense. I got it. I felt better. Until I got home.

And realized that no one is talking about him.

That the only chance I get to discuss our life is with Mark. And I lost it. I don't want him to be forgotten. I don't want to not talk about him. He's still such a part of me and my life. I still need to remember.

Major meltdown.

At 11 p.m. I did what I've tried not to do all this time.

Drink and dial.

I called my brother and just dumped. Crying hysterically, I told him what Mark said about the memory bank. About forgetting. About not talking about him.

John told me that he's wanted to talk about Rodg. Thinks about him all the time, but didn't want to upset me. That people *do* want to talk about him, but are afraid to. They realize how fragile I've been and don't want to push me. He said that Rodger was such a part of so many lives that a lot of people probably want to discuss him, talk about him, laugh about his jokes, remember him, but don't want to remind me.

I want to be reminded.

I want to know he was loved by so many. I need to talk about my husband. I need to talk about what I'm going through.

So much for easy highs and lows. So much for moving forward. I was right back to the bottom loop of the roller coaster when I finally crashed to sleep.

But I got up this morning and called my four closest friends. The ones who really knew him. The ones I trust with everything. I invited them to dinner. "I want to talk about Rodg," I told them. "I'm ready. I want to share. I want to hear you talk about him. I don't want to lose him. I don't want people to forget him."

And so we met. And talked. They asked questions about the stroke, the hospital, how I was really doing.

It was good to talk about him. To laugh at his foibles. To remember his jokes. To remember him.

I have one friend who can't talk about Rodg to this day without crying. She told me that when you walked into a room you just picked up on his energy. She gave me the best line of the evening.

"Rodger was a feeling."

It's not that there aren't days with extreme joy.

Those are when Katie's home. My beautiful daughter. She makes it back more than most of her friends, mainly because she's only an hour away.

I don't push, but I need my girl. I don't call and cry on her shoulder. She is having such a great time at college; she doesn't need a crazy, weepy mom on the other end of the line.

Maybe once a month I'll admit to her I'm having a tough day. But I don't go on and on about it. And I don't ever ask her to come home. She comes when she can and when she does I'm in heaven.

I spend way too much money. We do the mall run, the grocery run - all for "essentials!" She can't fit the clothes she has into her dorm closet but there's always a party or holiday, or event where she needs something new. So what the hey. I only have one, and might as well blow it on her. Plus, she makes me laugh. She'll text me jokes for Rodger's column - some so risqué I have to remind myself she's all grown up. But I love it. She's got her best friends at school with her, loves the campus, loves the independence.

She had to move on. I had to let her. This is her time to shine.

I've had mine. I did the college experience, summer in Europe, first boyfriend, first lover.

She needs to do the same.

There they were, lined up in a row facing the runway. The old World War II trainers.

They looked smaller than my SUV.

My friend at the Confederate Air Force had asked me to fly with him.

They had done such an amazing job at the memorial, and I'd written several stories about them since. He'd asked me to go up with them when they did a flyover and I said yes – I'd brave it!

You had to climb up the wing, throw your leg over the side and get in backwards, then turn around in this small, tight space, buckle down and hold on.

Once I was in, he said, "Come back out now and meet the guys." I demurred. Getting me into the damn plane once was enough. I wasn't risking life and limb to do it backwards. So I sat there, open to the sky, while he went back to the office.

There was no one else around. A few corporate jets landed at the other end of the runway, and I watched the elegant birds touch down. But there were no other people, and no cars. It was very quiet for an airport, and very peaceful.

I started to talk to Rodg. Told him that he would hate this (he actually hated small planes and heights) but would love that I was doing it. Told him this was in his honor, my WWII guy. I was doing it in part for him.

Across the runway something caught my eye.

A gold Cadillac turned onto the parkway, stopped behind the fence and just sat there. No one got out of the car. It didn't move. I blinked and looked again. It stayed there for a full five minutes then drove away when we took to the sky.

My heart flew higher than the plane that day.

Am I strong enough yet to let you go?

I worry sometimes about the gold Cadillacs, but I'm not ready to give them up.

I need a touchstone, something to remind me of you.

My practical daughter tells me that they're a crutch and eventually I'll stop seeing them. My sensitive, trippy sister in law says eventually I'll have to let you cross over.

But I don't know.

I don't know enough about the afterlife to know what's happening.

If by needing to see one everyday I'm keeping you earthbound I don't want it. But I don't think I'm strong enough yet to let them go.

I put on an act around other people. I cope, run a business, take care of mom, do my job, see my friends, entertain Thursdays, get out and about.

But only I know that it's all a charade. That underneath I crumble the minute I'm alone. That the phony shell of accomplishment is hiding the real self of shaky insecurity.

I don't want to be alone. I don't want to give up this connection to you.

I don't want to keep you trapped here on earth if you need to move on. I was strong enough in the hospital to tell you to fly. But not strong enough now.

Then it was about you. I could do anything to help you, to do what was right for you.

I now don't know what's right for me.

ॐ

Oh my love, I'm faking it so well.

Everyone says how wonderfully I'm doing.

They don't see me like this.

Night after night I cry on the way home. I'm back to the keening stage - the curled up in a ball position.

It's been eight months. It can't be. I cannot have lived eight months without you.

It seems like yesterday.

It seems like an eternity.

I look at my eighty year-old mother and think - I can't live to eighty. I can't do thirty years without you.

Because it doesn't hurt any less.

I don't miss you any less.

In fact, I probably miss you more now that the numbness has worn off. It's not a sharp pain but an ever-present ache, an emptiness I can't fill.

Everyone sees the competent, merry widow. The one who entertains, goes to the movies, smiles at community events.

The one who does it all.

Not the one who can't get out of bed on weekends. The one who doesn't want to get out of bed because that was our place, and there I can still pretend that you're next to me. I can hold the jacket to me and play make-believe under the cover of darkness.

In that game you're lying next to me. You've come to bed and held out your arms for me, smiling that special smile at me. You're holding me. You're making love to me. You're sleeping with me by your side.

If I don't turn over, if I don't wake up, it could still be real.

Because when my feet hit the floor, so does my soul.

Truth hits, and it's just me in the big room, the empty house, the solitary bed.

I get up to start the day, get dressed, go to work, and fake it all over again.

I don't know how long I can fool everyone.

I don't know how long I can fool myself.

ॐ

I went looking for a gun and found a vibrator.

They're both long, thin and end with a bang.

I had decided that living alone I should have protection. Rodger had a pistol somewhere buried in a closet. We'd hidden it up and away when Katie was a baby. But where?

I dug through the top shelves of my closet and found tons of old books, some photos and my first communion veil.

No gun, but a bag of gag gifts way in the back.

And lo and behold, what fell out but a long, narrow box. At first I wasn't sure what it was, but I turned it over and there in living color, bright lime green, was a dildo.

Given that the bag was filled with anti-aging pills, fake Viagra and the like, I figured this was a remnant of a birthday gift to be given or received. No clue. But there it was.

I pulled the thing out of the box and turned it over. It felt weird, like, well, plastic. It was sort of clammy but that may have been my imagination, or the revolting green color.

I touched the end and the damn thing started buzzing. I couldn't stop laughing. Here I am, fifty years old, sitting alone in my bedroom, with the Hulk's tool.

Well, it wasn't that big. But it did seem somewhat larger than what I was used to. And did I mention it was green?

What the hell now?

It was 10 a.m. so I stuck it in my end table drawer and kept working at the closet.

No gun, but that other phallic symbol stayed with me all day. I found myself chuckling at random times during the afternoon, thinking, "Am I really going to do this?"

When I finally got to bed, the ending was, well, anti-climactic.

The green color alone was enough to turn me off. I fiddled with it, so to speak, and it buzzed for a moment and then died. When I got down to actually using it, I was laughing so hard I gave up and watched the late news.

I told my girlfriends the story the next day and they were adamant. Get rid of it before Katie finds it.

Now, I don't think she'll be rifling my end table any time soon.

And until I find the gun, if there is an intruder, I can lob the green missile at them. It should distract them so much I can make a clean getaway.

I'm actually a crack shot.

When we lived in Arizona for a brief interlude my mother decided we should all have shooting lessons.

My sweet, tiny little mother in her diamonds and pearls can throw herself on the ground with a shotgun and blast the center out of a target.

A skill she hasn't needed much at Assistance League meetings.

But lessons we took, and we all learned to be comfortable handling a gun.

Now that I'm alone I want something more than the cat as back up.

In Big Bear this Christmas my brother brought up his pistol. We set up targets in the long backyard and fired away.

The sight was off slightly and I missed my first shot.

Correcting that, I blew the beer can and the pinecone off the table. Even he was impressed.

When I do find that damn gun, I'm going to take my friend Jerry's advice and load it with two blanks and one real bullet.

If I ever have an intruder, I can fire once in warning. I don't really want to kill anyone at that point. If they keep coming, they'll get a blank in the leg to scare the shit out of them.

If they insist on making my acquaintance, I'll give them the real thing.

They'll learn not to mess with an independent, menopausal suburban housewife.

Who happens to be packing.

I still cry when I come.

Orgasm – burst into tears.

Release follows release.

It's strange but I have to think it's pent up emotion and stress.

A masseuse once told me that muscle holds memory. That sometimes when she dug deep clients would cry out their buried feelings.

So for me it's one big muscle release. What pours out is memory, longing, sorrow, old joys, old wants.

It's not the same without Rodger.

My head knows it. My heart knows it, and my body knows it.

I ask Rodger to come to me in my dreams.

They are pretty vivid and I actually remember most of them. I can even get up in the middle of the night, go back to bed and back into the dream.

I don't see him as often as you would think. To fall asleep I block so many of the bad memories that I don't allow a lot of the good. But last night I asked him to visit, and he did.

I woke this morning realizing that not only did I see Rodg, but unlike most dreams where he is there but doesn't say anything, we had a long conversation. In the dream he asked me how I was coping, what I was doing without him, how I was doing without him. I don't remember my answers, but vividly remember his questions. He was worried about me.

It was so real.

I had told him that afternoon what I missed most was talking to him - and he heard me.

Because we talked all evening.

I got my wish.

I got my guy back, if only for a night.

The damndest things happen when someone dies.

People say the weirdest shit to you, or say nothing at all. I had one friend who said he couldn't talk to me for months because he didn't know what to say. Others tell you, "I know how you feel," and they don't, but at least they try.

Then there was – let's call her for the sake of protecting the guilty – Vanessa.

She was a former writer and friend of Rodger's. She was divorced and on the prowl, and I always thought she'd had a thing for him. She called me several months after his death, having just heard about it. She wanted to know all the details, and then said, "You know, I was after him for years. I would have gotten him if you hadn't gotten your claws into him."

Pardon me? This is how you open? This is what you say to the grieving fucking widow?

Okay sweetheart, here's the deal. If you were after him for years and nothing happened, wasn't that your first clue? You were friends, nothing more. Nothing happened. If he were interested, it would have happened long before I came on the scene.

She went on and on about how she knew she'd get together with

Rodger. I finally said, "Thanks for the call, got another coming in. Take care."

And then just laughed. I wasn't even offended. I was still so raw that it rolled off me. And I knew better.

Rodg used to say when I went to garage sales or shopping with friends, "Don't worry, I'll just call Vanessa for company." He knew she had the hots for him. But he was kind, and gentle, and never encouraged it.

I wasn't as gentle, and basically hung up on the bitch.

She deserved it.

I'd finally done it. Moved forward with the paper. Moved into the twenty first century.

The paper was uploaded virtually to the printer. Gone were the messenger costs. Gone were the sloppy art boards. Gone were the old days.

I was telling Rodg all about it.

I told him how we'd thrown the boards away. Filed the ads we might need, but probably wouldn't, in the future.

The bare walls and empty light table glared stark white in the office. They had no use now. Those days were over.

I explained the transition. Told him though it made my life easier it was so hard to let yet another piece of us go.

I used to love our Thursdays. We laid out the paper, wrote stories together, searched for news, built something together. We fought over placement, layout, stories, ads, what deserved page one, and what was relegated to the back. It was what we did together. It was our livelihood, our life, our work, our creation.

And when Thursday was done we'd celebrate on the patio with wine and cheese. Time together not arguing over headlines. Time together reviewing the news. Time together.

This new digital production will cut my workweek in half. I can spend more time writing. More time on me. Less time looking for logos, pictures, lost ads.

But it's the time with Rodger I will miss. Those hours in the office looking for the right photo. Laughing at the possible headlines. Fighting over layout. Who would write which story. What got in. What got trashed. Moving in sync as we put the whole thing together from start to finish.

It was what we did. It's who we were.

So I cried as I told him the news. How we'd done it. How we'd done it all digitally. How I missed him. How he'd hate it.

But I still think about what he would write. What he would think deserves front page. What funny headline to put in. How he'd handle a story. What jokes to fill up his column.

So even if we're not working side by side he's still a part of it.

Even if he's not online, he's there.

Forget the apple.

I had a masseuse who once told me that an orgasm a day was the way to stay healthy. Gets all the juices flowing, heart rate going, blood moving.

My "one a day" time is certainly over, but I must say that when I do get one in, I have a much better day following.

Not only do I feel closer to Rodger, I just feel better . Those endorphins kick in. I sleep more soundly, wake up happier and ready to take on the world.

After sex most men fall asleep.

Most women could run a marathon.

So I take that energy and go run the papers. And I do it with a smile.

It's almost April. Time to shed the heavy layers.

I'm ready to deal with Rodger's closet now.

I've taken what I want from it. I still sleep with his travel jacket. His favorite baseball hat is perched on the pencil holder next to my computer. I saved the Italia sweatshirt he got when we conceived Katie. His Fresno State sweatshirt. The sweater he and I both wore 'round the world. The plaid shirt I bought him in the Cotswolds. The CIA shirt a friend gave him that he treasured. His ridiculously large silver dollar belt buckle.

I e-mailed the kids asking them what they wanted, and gave them the deadline of Easter to come get it. I have plenty of memories, mementoes, things that were special to us. If there is something in particular that means something to them, I want to hand it over.

I'm ready. Most of it is just clothes. If someone can use them, great. A lot of it was never worn. A lot of it really can't be worn by anyone but else - most of his shirts have his initials on them. The pants are too big for any of the boys. The beautiful Harris Tweed jackets from England and Ireland are special, and will fit one of them.

I already gave Steve the tux. None of the other boys are big black tie attendees. I gave John the black plaid jacket. He'd always told Rodg he had the same coat in college - his "lucky" coat. After that I couldn't see anyone but him getting lucky in it.

So it can all go - to the boys, to charity, to someone who will use it.

I've gone through it all. I've held it to me. I've smelled every piece hoping to find him. Sorted it into piles. The things that resonated I've kept.

I wasn't ready to do this at Christmas. I didn't want to make it more emotional than it already was. I had bought each of the kids a cuffed shirt from Brooks Brothers, and gave them each a set of Rodger's cufflinks. I kept one pair for myself.

Katie's home this weekend, and I told her to see if there's anything she wants. She already nabbed a sweatshirt that she sleeps in, one that meant something of her daddy to her.

There are four watches - two gold Hamiltons, one from California Newspaper Publisher's Association with the inkwell and pen engraved on it. Marc wants that one. There's a gold Mickey Mouse watch I think Doug would like. I'm going to keep the Hamilton tank watch I gave Rodger. If mine ever fails I'll have his on my wrist.

They are just things. But they are things that meant something to him, to us. I want to pass them on to people that meant something to him and to us. His children. My guys.

ॐ

Rodg loved his cowboy boots, and looked damn good in them.

One of the boys asked for them. But I can't let them go, and am pretty sure can't tell him the reason.

Rodger had left work early one day, and made it home before me. I pulled up hours later, tired, cranky and done for the day. I put my key in the lock and he opened the door. Greeted me wearing the cowboy boots.

Nothing else.

Needless to say, I was cranky no more.

Those boots are going nowhere. They've been taken out of the closet, polished, shined, and sit in a place of honor in the library.

And only I know why.

Victoria is opening up.

I think the six months has given Rodger's oldest time to heal as well. None of us are completely centered, but we're getting there. She hasn't wanted to talk about her father all this time.

I met her for a drink at her apartment early January.

She had the football game on mute as a concession to my visit. Vik is a complete football fanatic - she comes alive from September to Super Bowl.

We talked work. Newspaper. Kate. The bro's. What's up with her. And of course, football. Actually, she talked football; I nodded at what I assumed were appropriate places.

She threw into the conversation that what she misses most about Rodg is calling him in the middle of a game and talking "football swag."

The give and take of scores. Arguing calls. Bashing refs. Gloating over team wins.

I didn't say much. This is the first time she's volunteered any comment about her father. I let her go on and just nodded and said, "he loved when you called."

When I got home I pulled out his Fresno State sweatshirt. She deserved it. She needed it. I'm not the football fan.

I'm not the one who needs to feel close to her dad again.

She does.

I tied a ribbon and note around it, boxed it up and mailed it to her.

The note said simply "You can still talk football to him. I know he's there, and I know he's listening."

And I know that they both need it still.

ह

I gave my Valentine a red, red rose.

My Valentine gave me a candle that says "Don't Stop."

Believing? Living?

"Well," I was told, "Given the name of your book you'd know what a massage candle that says 'don't stop' means."

I couldn't stop laughing. Valentine's Day was spent with my friend Lisa, whose husband had just left for a job in DC.

We two singles went to the see the movie "Valentine's Day" - which actually opens with Hector Elizondo driving a gold Cadillac - then out for sushi.

The next night Kate and I drove down to San Diego to see the boys. It took five hours but it was five hours with my girl. We talked, she slept, I talked to Rodg about our beautiful baby.

I always love going to the kids' houses. And this time I saw everywhere. His caricature from the paper was on display in an office. The picture of him and his boys goofing off at the Renaissance Faire was on a bookshelf. A picture of Rodg, Vic and Bruce was on the table in the front hall.

He was loved, and remembered, and cherished still.

And all weekend I was loved and cherished. Doug and Michelle gave each of the "girls" red tulips for Valentine's. A beautiful dinner. A priceless evening with those I love.

And on the way back I told Rodg all about it. Talked to him in my head while Katie read.

It's a holiday about lovers, and love.

I still had mine - and so much more.

Spring has sprung, and with it hope.

There is new growth on the hills the house. A tiny baby bunny is nibbling his way through the yard outside my window every morning.

Life goes on.

And on mornings like this, I know I can too.

It's been ten months, and as the months have rolled by I've rolled up and down with them. This month I'm up.

I had a great dinner with friends last night, and then a "date" with Rodger. These late night forays into self-gratification aren't regular, but when I can bring him back into my head and my bed I wake up a happier, more positive person. I sleep the sleep of the content and can face the day and what it brings.

I've got the paper and the bank in better shape this week. My sister and I are taking mom to the mountains on Friday. Kate will be home Sunday for the February birthday celebrations.

I have things to look forward to.

I wake up and say good morning to Rodger's picture, and kick-start my daily routine.

Today, I myself spring out of bed with a little more hope. Maybe it's the sunshine. Maybe it's the decent night's sleep. Maybe it's the passage of time. I just know I feel better today, and am going to run with it.

I almost lost it, but didn't.

I just stayed cool and smiled.

I'm not emotional every time I talk about Rodger anymore.

I told Kate about giving her sister the Fresno State sweatshirt. Asked her if I thought it was the right thing to do.

She said Vik has been so closed up, so wound tight about Rodg, that this was good. She agreed that if she's started talking about him she's starting to heal.

And so I had the courage to ask Kate, "Why did you pick the red sweatshirt to take with you to school?" I couldn't put any real significance to it.

"That was Dad's tennis shirt," she said. "He wore it every time we played tennis together."

My little varsity ace. My grown up girl. She has her own memories of her daddy and keeps them close.

While inside I cried and bled a little for times shared, times never again to be experienced, I only smiled at her and said, "That's lovely."

And let it be.

She's not the only one growing up.

At eighty, Rose remembers the best make-up sex she ever had.

She has been a widow ten years.

I knew her husband Nat, and the two of them guided me through the first years of my business. They also had a love affair that started young, and worked together up until Nat's death. The two of them knew Rodger almost as long as I did, and also loved him.

So when I have lunch with her I don't have to hold back.

I can cry. Laugh. Share stories.

I don't have to tell her I'm doing fine. She knows me, knew us, and knows the truth.

I value her wisdom. I asked her how she survived for ten years without him. I'm at ten months and not sure how I will live without him another six months, let alone six years, or sixteen.

Rose said that you can't look to the future. It's surviving day to day. She's a great example. She still works every day and is planning a birthday bash/fundraiser for the whole community.

She gave me the words I cling to.

"It doesn't get better - it gets different."

I can believe that. It's not a platitude or meant to appease. It's the truth. It really doesn't get better. I haven't stop missing him any less, or loving him any less.

But it's no longer a shock.

Disbelief has turned to dull ache. It's not an open wound anymore, but an ever-present pain that I've learned to live with. Whenever I'm reminded of something about Rodger, it's like the pain intensifies. The dull point of the knife sticking in my side jabs a little deeper.

It's like having a paper cut.

I'm walking around with a slice out of me, but I've learned to carry the pain. It's only when something caustic reminds me that it stings.

Or when I push on it myself. I want to remember. I want to cry. I need to let out all this bottled up emotion. So I wait until I get home to pour salt on it. To dig up the night of the stroke, the long days at the hospital, the last minutes when I held him.

Rose told me when those thoughts come along - remember the first time we kissed. A favorite trip. The birth of Katie.

So I do. I push the bad memories aside, and let the amazing ones flood in. Our trip to Costa Rica. Our bench in Paris. Our baby. Days spent on the patio. Nights in our bed.

And I can go on, for another hour. Another day.

Michael is dying.

I know it, and his wife knows it.

We're keeping the community at bay and telling them there's no change.

My friend the community leader, the business exec, the crazy, loud guy I've known for almost thirty years is fading away.

And it brings back all sorts of tough memories.

Michael had a heart attack, and is now in a coma in a Palm Spring hospital. Eerily similar to ten months ago.

Those that know me well have called to ask how I'm taking it.

They know we're close. They know this hits close to home.

Heart attack. Stroke. Palm Springs' hospital. Coma. Waiting. Watching. Keeping the wolves and gossip hounds at bay.

But I'm doing okay.

It's not Rodg. It's not me.

I can do something this time. I can help Jen by telling the world to stay away. Telling them the situation is the same. Call me, or her assistant, for information.

Don't call the wife. Don't go to the hospital. Don't bother her while she makes the toughest decisions of her life.

Already the rumors have swirled out of control.

It happened with Rodg.

One person calls a friend, sends an email, tells another. And the whole community is aflame with the news. The questions. The "what happened?" The wanting to be part of someone else's train wreck.

I had friends who found out Rodger died on the Internet. I never got a chance to call them because someone else already had.

Part of it is being part of a tight community.

Part of it is people wanting to make the drama their own.

I lived through it. I fought the intrusion. I turned the phone calls, emails, inquiries over to my sister while I dealt with the doctors, the decisions, the death of the person closest to me.

I shut out the world for one week.

This wasn't their tragedy. This wasn't their loss.

In reality, it was. Rodger was, and Michael is, a part of their gestalt, their business life, their community.

But in those last moments, it comes down to family.

I made the decision to pull the plug, to let Rodger die with dignity.

Jen will have to do the same.

And if I can give her the space, the quiet, to do that, I will.

I won't make it all about me. It's not. So I can handle it. I can imagine the same situation, the same story, the same ending.

But I'm not living it.

By answering the calls, buffering the intrusions, I'm just trying to help her live through it. Since I already have.

¿&

I needed comfort food.

After this long week with Michael and Jen, fighting demons of the past, I needed pasta and a glass of wine.

For the second time in weeks I went to our favorite Italian restaurant.

Only one reason was for the food.

Another was that I could sit there in our corner booth and see Rodger across the table. I could talk to him in my head, watching him eat Spaghetti Bolognese.

Creatures of habit, we two. I still order the Adagio salad and capellini cecca. A glass of red for him, white for me.

And talk. For an hour or more when the paper was done, we were done in, and loved just sitting across the booth from each other and catching up.

So today I went back. To the restaurant, to our booth, to those times.

And with some tears, but more smiles, I saw you there, telling stories, joking with the waiter, smiling over at me.

When I left the owner pulled out Rodger's obituary from next to the register to show me. He'd cut it out and kept it.

I'm not the only one there who remembers.

Jen is going to make it.

Not only did she text me Thursday to see how my day was going - in the middle of all her craziness she knew it was a tough week - but she called last night laughing.

"I know what we can give up for Lent!"

"I give up."

"We're guaranteed to make it forty days. This is one we won't blow. Not like wine, where we give up halfway through the first week!"

"Tell me."

Cracking up, we both said at the same time, "Sex!"

She said, "That's it. We're going to be so good this Lent. We won't renege on our resolution. We can make it the full forty."

This one I know I can keep. This resolution won't get broken.

Hell, it hasn't for eleven months. What's six weeks more?

I will survive.

I didn't know that in the beginning.

All those baby steps, day by long day, led me here.

I watch the kids pile in their cars following a visit. We are a family still.

Flesh of my flesh.

Flesh of his flesh.

Their progeny.

The next generation. And the next after that.

Rodger lives on in his five children, and their children. His wit, his charm, his quick mind, I see in them.

It is a new year. I will face it sustained by their visits, their calls, their love.

I will always see Rodger in them. The way Doug tells a joke. The way Katie tilts her head at me. Marc's smile. I will always carry him in my heart, my head. He's a piece of all of us. I have my guys. My girls. Myself. I have enough for now.

Someone told me the only way my story would end was for me to meet someone. Not true. I don't need that to go on. I only had to meet my demons, my fears, my needs.

I did it myself. With a lot of help from Rodg.

Hospitals are tough gigs.

I spent the night in the ER with my elderly friend Louise. There is nothing I wouldn't do for her – she's like a second mother to me. So I spent the night curled up in a hospital chair, something I know all too well how to do.

But that confinement actually freed me.

The doctor told us they wanted to do a carotid artery scan on her, which upset me.

I have spent months obsessing over what I could have done for Rodg. A scan, more check ups, better diet, more monitoring.

So I asked my brother, "Could a scan have saved Rodger's life?" His left artery had showed "some occlusion" according to his hospital report.

But he set my mind at ease. With his a-fib, and need for Coumadin, he was a time bomb waiting to happen. It could have come from any direction, he said. So a scan may have showed some problems, and they could have put in a stint (which Rodg would have hated) but it wouldn't necessarily have prevented the stroke. He had too much going on, and I couldn't have covered it all.

"Besides," he said. "He lived beyond all expectations with his condition, and lived it well. Stop beating yourself up."

I'm the queen of guilt. I worry things like a bone, agonizing and over-thinking issues.

But Steve reminded me of what I did right.

"He died happy. You guys had a wild ride the night before. It's every man's dream, to go out after sex."

So he made me laugh.

Made me let go of the guilt, and remember the good.

More women shave their legs for the gynecologist than for Valentine's Day. It's true, according to a study done by Schick.

I believe it, as I actually shaved my legs on Friday.

A new high.

I'm blond so you really wouldn't notice, and who's looking? But I was getting a massage and didn't want to show up with prickly legs.

When Rodg was alive I was never the hirsute hobo I am today.

I was always perfectly clean-shaven or waxed – all over – and it was all for him.

Now it's time to do it for me.

The closest I feel to Rodger is when I bring him back to bed with me.

It's just the two of us in my mind, in my hands, in my heart.

I thought about him all day today. For some reason I traced his body over and over in my head.

From that silver hair, the craggy James Coburn face, the sharp but soft cheekbones, the hairy chest, to the lean hips, long legs, strong, beautiful cock.

When I got to bed I was ready, I was primed, to think about him and nothing else.

I played, I came, and slept the deepest sleep I'd slept in months.

And awoke smiling.

I never thought of myself as a cougar.

Not sure whether to be amused or appalled.

Every Monday after writing group my friend Jerry and I (or as we call ourselves, Jules and Julia) cook dinner from Julia Childs' cookbook. We hit the market, start cooking and have dinner ready when his wife gets home. Sometimes it's the three of us, sometimes there's a whole gang we've put to work chopping, dicing and cooking with us.

Steak au poivre. Poulet a la port. Boeuf Bourgignon. We're working our way through the food groups.

But one of Patty's friends was upset.

"You leave your husband home all afternoon alone with your single friend?"

She just laughed.

"My best friend and my husband. I don't think so."

Now, it has happened in the annals of television and Peyton Place.

But here's the deal.

The only person I want to sleep with is currently unavailable, and will be in perpetuity.

So I think Jerry's safe.

Plus I did have another friend ask me point blank if there was anyone I knew I would sleep with.

I went down the list. First off, I don't have any single or divorced male friends who aren't gay. So that's out.

Then I went through the married list. I really gave it some thought - sort of like the Monty Python sketch - "no, no yes...no, no yes."

Really, it was all no's. They are wonderful men, but I don't poach. And they're not Rodg. I may be so horny I'm climbing the walls, but I'm not about to climb into bed with a married man. Or any man right now.

I love Jerry. But I'm not going to jump his bones.

The only thing that will get boned on a Monday afternoon will be a duck.

Besides, I've hit a dry spell.

For months I was so horny I couldn't stand it. Now, a year later, it's tapered off.

Without my partner, without Rodg, it's not as compelling. Maybe because I'm not as emotional. The extreme highs and lows have subsided, and along with them my libido. I've calmed down a lot.

I hate the complacency.

I hate to think I've lost that part of me that was so vital, so excitable, so much a part of our relationship. I miss sex but I'm not driven to have it as much, even with myself.

About once a week I'll think, yes! And out comes the KY and the fantasies. But it's an effort, and it's just not the same without him. But I try, and most of the time can get off, fall into a deep sleep, and wake up raring to go.

But getting me going seems to take more effort these days. Maybe I'm just focused on other things. Work, paying bills, organizing the house. Maybe I'm just getting older. But menopause didn't slow me down with Rodg, work never stopped me from jumping him any chance I'd get. I wanted him all the time, loved him all the time.

I haven't dried up. I still can get excited. I still can feel, get wet, ready and randy. But for whom? For what? I miss my guy. I miss Rodg. I miss his body, his smell, his voice, his touch. As much as I pretend, it's not him who's touching me. And it's not the same.

I think more than my body, it's my emotions that have dried out.

I'm trying to be alone - and be okay with it.

I'm a very social person – Thursdays, dinners, plays. But I'm trying to enjoy my alone time and not fear it.

I invited friends to big Bear, but went up a day early to open the house, de-winterize and have some down time after a crazy workweek.

I don't go upstairs where Rodger had his stroke unless I want to cry. Instead I celebrated the so many happy times we spent here. Walking the lake, shopping at the village, finding something at his favorite Pendleton store. There are so many good memories to balance out the bad.

He always wanted to buy me something. A sweater, a pair of red lacy earrings. A sexy bra. We loved prowling the small shops, the used bookstore. He could talk to any one and would chat up the storeowners about business, traffic, life in Big Bear, all while I shopped.

We'd return to the cabin, sit on the back porch facing the mountain, have wine, and talk, talk, talk. We'd make love tucked away from the world.

So I made it up the hill about 8 p.m., ordered Chinese food and had a glass of wine. I read for a few hours and let the silence settle in around me.

I was by myself, but surrounded by good memories, wasn't alone.

I need to be Mommy sometimes.

My grown up girl still needs me. She emails and texts. Sometimes just for me I have to sign the emails Mommy – not a lot, but once in a while I still have to be that close. That personal. It probably drives my nineteen-year-old crazy, but she puts up with a lot more from me now, and understands. I'm sure she knows I need it more than she does. But that's okay. We've gone to hell and back in the last year.

I know she thinks about her dad. She has a tribute to him on her Facebook page. She doesn't speak about him much, but she misses him. We all do. She talks constantly to her brothers and sister, her aunts, sisters in law and more on the Internet. They have a connection. They need a connection.

Rodger's death was hard on all of us. I guess I just emote the most. I think the kids all try to take care of me. The boys call a lot. Vik emails me.

We've all been hit by lightening.

We've all had to reassess our lives, our goals, our purpose. Rodger was our anchor. The stable, good Fresno guy with down home values we all needed. The family man, the rock, the solid person we all leaned on, until he was gone. I still lean on him. Whether that's good or bad

I don't know. But he's there for me. I know it. I feel it. And I've told all the kids about the Cadillacs. They either believe me or humor me. It doesn't matter either way. It gets me through the days. It gets me through the night.

I have to be proud of myself. I'm making it day to day. I don't curl up in a ball that often anymore. I still cry a lot in my car, but it's a rolling sadness, not as much a punch in the gut.

I can't say I'm happy, but I'm not so miserable.

I'm learning to live with me.

I'm learning to live for me.

I was so used to taking care of a husband, child, house, business, family, that this is the first time in twenty five years I'm taking a hard, long look at myself.

The grief counselor said now is the time, after eleven months of mourning, that I ask, "What the hell do I want to do now?"

I decided a few things.

Once I'm past taxes, I want to concentrate on writing.

I've decided to take myself to Paris for our anniversary and Rodger's birthday. It will be a difficult week at best, so I'd rather be sad in the city of lights. I'd rather mourn my loss away from everyone else.

I want to sit at a small cafes and write. Spend hours in the garden of the Rodin museum. Take a notepad to the Pont d'Alma and sit next to the Seine.

It's a rite of passage.

It's proof I can exist alone.

It's a goal, and a reason for being.

It's my next step in this independent life I've been given. I didn't choose to be alone, but I can choose how to spend that time alone.

So I did it. I took off.

I love Paris in the springtime.

The old song rings true, because my love *is* here, with every step I take. Walking down Rue Cler. Looking in the windows of Boucherie Roger. Laughing with the crepe man. Making love in the small bed with the window open to the Eiffel Tower's radiance.

I took a long walk in the rain today. I know Le Septieme as well as my own neighborhood. Noted the new stores. Peeked into old favorites.

Dropped into La Terrasse for dinner.

I expected to be lonely.

I am not.

I expected to be sad.

I'm happier than I've been in a long time.

Like Paris, I feel like I have been liberated from months of oppression and sorrow.

I can breathe here.

I slept deeply and soundly last night. The sleep of the innocent.
I feel like I have been reborn.

Here, I am not a widow.

Here, I am not a publisher.

Here, I am not a daughter.

Here I have no responsibilities. I shed them when I got on that plane.

I simply get to be.

Do what I want, when I want.

It is a peaceful feeling. I wander the back streets of Paris and detour into little gardens. I take my time with everything. I am simply an observer. I can sit at a café and take forever to drink a café crème, and make up stories about the people around me.

At the flea market I lingered over old prints, and bought funny old postcards to send to friends back home. I haggled over a silver tray I really didn't need, and didn't buy, but it was fun to try out my French and bargain like a true Frenchwoman.

Not sure whether I am up to facing the Eiffel Tower and my memories head on, sitting at "our" bench on the Champs de Mars yet. I may stay in my room and just watch it twinkle on the hour.

That's my new speed. There is no need to rush anything. I have an entire week of this, and today is only day one.

As Katie would say, today was a good day.

I bought hyacinths this morning. It was such a fabulously spring, French thing to do!

They make my room smell like Paris. I sit at the window with the computer perched on the old radiator and write. I can see the top of the Eiffel Tower peeking over the rooftops. Paris is spread out under my open shutters.

I feel like F. Scott Fitzgerald or George Sand. Instead of Chopin playing in the background though, I have my favorite CD, "In the Mood," of old favorites playing while I write. I may have to go buy an Edith Piaf CD just to stay in that mood.

It's almost April in Paris, and now it smells like it in my hotel room.

I'm doing what the grief counselor told me to do, which is make the moment mine.

The flowers were a start.

Here I sit, tracing the step of famous writers for inspiration. Les Deux Magots. Saint Germain de Pres, a la Place Sartre-Beavoir. Home away from home for Hemingway and Fitzgerald. Seems like you can't go anywhere in Paris without running into those two.

Of all things, at the corner is an accordion player.

Next to me an older man waves to a much younger woman crossing the street. An assignation? Meanwhile an older woman has lunch with her dog. C'est la vie...

For me, 'tis a feast. A millefuille salad of tomate and goat cheese. A glass of wine and the inevitable baguette.

Breakfast was the most delish – the thick, creamy chocolate chaud and macaroons at Laduree, where I stopped on my shopping tour down the Champs Elysee – buying coffee and macaroons there for Kate's Easter basket, a candle from the Crillon Hotel for Vik (the best gift shop in Paris), and perfume for Mom at Guerlain. It is certainly one of the oldest and most beautiful stores in Europe with its gold fittings marble and gilt mirrors. I came here to buy L'heure Blue for mom, the perfume her mother always wore.

I buy some for myself, perhaps channeling that great beauty whose life was a story unto itself until she died tragically of alcoholism at thirty-one.

I want to channel the beauty part, and avoid the unhappy ending.

ॐ

I saw Tina today. She has been the housekeeper at the hotel as long as Rodg and I have been coming here. Thirty years? Our conversation is always limited as she speaks no English and I have limited French. Usually I ask "Ca va?" and she rattles off a litany of complaints about too much work, too many tourists, etc. I get about half of it. I know that the hotel owner is "en vacances." Her ex is still running his singles bar in Montmartre. Her knees hurt and she's too old for this. I got that much. She asked me, "Ca va?" and I could only reply "Comme si, comme ca. Je suis seul ici."

"I'm here alone."

She gave me a hug and said "La vie n'est pas juste."

She's right.

Life's not fair. But I'm learning to make it balance out a little.

And Paris is a damn good start.

Shakespeare and Co.

I bought a Hemingway classic at Sylvia Beach's old bookstore, where all the great literary lights gathered in Paris. To this day they still give rooms to struggling authors. I wonder if I qualify? The bookstore is full of English books, funny old tiled sayings imbedded the floor, curious people prowling the aisles. I looked at a lot of great old classics, and decided Hemingway's paean to Paris was meant to be. Then I sat at a small cafe to read it.

He sat here for hours – I stayed a little under one. The goal was the same. To be inspired in Paris. By its people, smells and sounds.

I can see the bouqinistes with their prints, dirty postcards, old maps. I can see Notre Dame, the river, the beginnings of the Latin Quarter.

Watch the tourists and not feel like one.

ε&

My first bite into a baguette. Mon dieu! The French do bread better than anyone on the planet.

This is not going to be a low cal trip. Because as Hemingway said, Paris is a moveable feast.

And it is all spread out like a gourmet smorgasbord in front of me.

Staying on Rue Cler is living with temptation. The cobblestone street is one of the most charming places I've ever been. It is an open market, so the fromagerie is across from the hotel, the boucherie is next door. The wine store beckons, as does the art deco patisserie down the block. I can wander for hours from stall to stall and into the little shops.

I spend an entire morning picking a new cheese. Deciding between the patés. Looking at the fruit, laid out in perfect rows we used to call "food porn."

It is that decadent.

It is that tempting.

It is that I cannot resist.

Dinner tonight is a pate de campagne avec poivres, Brillat Savarin cheese, brie, cornichons and a baguette. I am truly a terrible girl and bought myself some French butter to slather on the baguette as well. And for dessert, mon petit choux, a mille feuille pastry filled with cream.

At Repaire de Bacchus our old friend is there. When we made our second trip within a year, he said he remembered us from before, and we "were thirsty then!"

I am still thirsty, and found a fabulous little French white - not too dry, not too fruity, simplemente "parfait" to accompany my picnic meal.

I also snuck an almond croissant into my room for breakfast tomorrow. I plan to sleep in, nibble my pastry, make some tea, and wake up to the world slowly. The Eiffel Tower out my window greets me every morning like a beacon. Paris is waiting!

There are museums to see, rivers to cross, shops to peruse, and Croque Monsieur's waiting for me at lunch.

A bientot! It rains hard every night, but the days are warm and sunny. I wake up to a Paris cleaned and scrubbed for me to explore.

Tonight I watched the sun set behind the Eiffel Tower.

The room is awash in honey gold light.

Last night my room was filled with thoughts of Rodger.

I went to sleep remembering our nights here together. How he felt sleeping next to me, in my arms. I could actually see him in my dreams. That silver hair, strong arms, chest hair, underarms. I touched him head to toe and remembered him touching me. So many nights we lay in this room, in this bed, making love to the ambient light of the tower. I let him come to me, and I came again.

I slept 'till eleven the next day.

Can I rhapsodize about cheese? The Brie from the fromagerie is running off the plate. The Brillat Savarin lives up to its name – soft and creamy, just sharp enough.

I have so few sensual pleasures left I am savoring this plate of melt in your mouth delights. So many cheeses and so little time ….

I did pick up a new Stilton today, along with some different patés.

I'm seriously thinking of not visiting another restaurant and just living on cheese and wine selected from the wine steward at Repaire de Bacchus. I teach him English each time I go in, and he picks out a new and better wine for me each time.

A perfect "mariage Française!"

I was in my room shooting pictures of the Eiffel Tower at sunset, when the CD played "Moon River."

That's when I lost it.

I miss my other drifter, off to see the world.

We had gone everywhere together.

I'm off by myself now to see the world. I'm crossing it "in style," but doing it alone.

I'm sure the neighbors across the way thought I was ready to jump.

Here's this crazy lady standing on the bed with a camera pointed out the open window, tears pouring down her face.

I captured the sunset, but lost the sense of contentment I'd had up until now.

I miss my Huckleberry friend.

Every corner told a story.

On every corner Rodg told the story.

I finally figured out one of the things I miss most.

It took a while, but standing in front of the Arc de Triomphe I knew. It was Rodger's explanation of the war effort. My World War II historian always gave us background on what we were seeing. And in Europe it's on every corner.

The bullet holes in the Prefecture of Police, which was used by the Resistance. The chipped bricks at the Crillon Hotel, which Hitler made his Paris headquarters. The lack of a tribute to the Americans at the Arc, where Rodg would rant and rave about how they all would be speaking German if not for us – but still no monument.

I learned so much from him. I read *Is Paris Burning?* - where von Choltitz knew Hitler was going mad and wouldn't blow up the bridges of Paris. I thought of that every time I crossed the Pont Neuf.

He had encyclopedic knowledge of the war and imparted it to me. I am fuzzy on details of Vietnam but can tell you about how the French used the Metro System in Paris to outwit the Nazis. It was his passion. When we traveled half our journey was going to the war museums, the concentration camps, the memorials. We all learned, and loved it.

It made where we were real.

The people, the monuments, the stories.

In Poland Katie and her friend said the best thing they did was visit Auschwitz. It was certainly the most difficult, but also the most poignant, the most important, the most emotional.

Rodg gave us that.

He brought history, and our travels, to life.

Another country heard from.

I scheduled a massage at the spa down the street. I was sore from the plane and all the walking, and just thought I'd kick start my week relaxed and happy.

Who knew how happy?

The masseuse spoke no English, and my French doesn't extend to spa niceties.

She gestured for me to take off my clothes and put on a little cloth g-string. Got that. Same as at home.

I lay on my stomach and she started massaging my legs. Seemed to be strong, but going a little high up the thigh. But ah well, this is France.

They have better lingerie and fewer hang-ups.

Great massage. Very mellow.

I turned over on my back and she did the front of my legs.

Then she rattled off a question and asked "Pas de problem?"

No clue what she asked but figured she wanted to rub my stomach, which they don't usually do at home. No problem, I told her.

Not only did she rub my stomach, but basically started right above the bikini line, over my stomach, over and around both breasts up to my neck.

So that was what she was asking.

She kept rubbing circles around and on my breasts down to my stomach.

No one had touched me in so long. I didn't want to appear anxious – was a little concerned that my nipples might get hard. But I didn't want to look like an unsophisticated American so I didn't open my eyes and just went with it.

It was really all very clinical, just very up close and personal.

But damn, it felt good.

When I went to pay the woman at the desk asked if everything was all right.

I just smiled and told her "Pas de problem."

For some reason Harvey Weinstein and I were making a movie last night.

I was feeling a little blue after writing about Rodger all day. I went to sleep asking him – begging him – to come to me in my dreams. I can only deal with so much of the ethereal and then I need to see him.

Poor guy. I have really wackadoo dreams, and he was probably trying to figure out where to fit into them.

But gotta give it to him, he showed up.

Do I know Harvey? No. Do I make movies? No.

So I can see Rodg with his familiar "God damn it, Mary Kathleen. What now?"

But he showed up in the dream. He drove me home from the set. What???

Doesn't matter.

He heard me.

He showed up.

He makes me laugh, even now.

The Kiss.

Rodin's famous sculpture.

Two lovers frozen together, joined together.

The marble cast is a life-size portrait of love. A naked man and woman at their most intimate. Captured that way forever.

I don't want to move out of that pose, that frame.

And I don't want to forget that feeling, that intense love portrayed in bronze. I certainly don't want to kiss another.

I had my love affair, my moment. Now, it also is frozen in time.

I told my sister when I die I want to be cremated, and my ashes mixed with Rodger's.

So we too, will be holding each other for eternity.

❧

I ordered up an "Orgasmo." How could I not?

It was too early to sit in my room, however much I love my little retreat. So I sat at a new café on Rue Cler to people watch 'till the sun went down.

The beauty of Paris is that they let you sit and sit and sit with one drink and a carafe of water.

I watched little French children in school uniforms, old couples arm in arm, and shoppers perusing the stalls.

Looking over the carte de vin I couldn't resist.

Too few and far between.

The Orgasmo was basically a Cosmopolitan with blackcurrant juice, and it was to die for.

Truly worth waiting for.

Aren't they all?

My pilgrimage has finally brought me here.

Le Champs de Mars.

Our bench under the Eiffel Tower.

I see families, students, lovers, all enjoying the day – and each other - under the shadow of the tower.

But today, really, there are no shadows.

I thought I'd be sad but am so peaceful. I had twenty-five years of this, twenty-five years of memories, picnics, playtime with Kate, friends and family.

All here at this small green, French bench. We would spread out a picnic and sit facing each and just rejoice in being together. Being in Paris, being lovers, being our little family, being part of something bigger than ourselves with our friends at our side.

The sun warmed the park and I could see through the tower's span to the Museum of Man, Kate's favorite carousel, the bridge over the Seine.

All good memories, ones not everyone has. So I am blessed.

While I was sitting there a man walked by, picked a ring out of the dust and showed me what he had found. A wedding band, he said.

Even though I was probably being scanned I was amused. "Doesn't fit at all," he said, and gave it to me.

"Do you have any coins for a sandwich?" he asked. Now I knew it was a scam. But it meant something to me and I went along with it. Gave him four Euros and took the ring.

I'll leave that gold circle on the bench when I leave.

'Cause my life circled back here. My memories came full circle here.

And maybe someone will find it, on our bench, and have hope and faith. In marriage, in miracles, in memories.

Because I do.

＊

I'm back on my knees.

I caught the tail end of mass at Notre Dame today. Lit candles in the little local church on Rue Cler. That one was tough.

I prayed to God to take care of my guy. That's all I want. To know he's okay. No one was in the little stone church so I knelt there, quietly sobbing.

I've sort of gone back to church. Sort of, because I went to mass before I left home, but it's not a regular thing. I stopped completely when Rodg died.

Don't know if I was angry with God, or just numb.

I prayed so hard in the hospital and the worst happened, so all my prayers were for naught. So I thought I'd at least try – hit a few churches in Paris and try to get some feeling back.

I always lit candles when we traveled. Churches are big tourist stops in any major city, part of the itinerary. Rodg always gave me coins to drop in then waited for me. He prayed silently too. Not a Catholic, but certainly a much better Christian than I.

Who thought I'd be lighting candles for him?

Happy anniversary, baby.

Today would have been our twenty-second wedding anniversary. I flew through London to commemorate it there. I knew I shouldn't be sad, but when they printed out my tube ticket with the date flat across the front, it floored me. I just stood stock still in the middle of the busy station, silent tears overflowing.

I can forget. I can move forward. Then it hits me like a ton of bricks.

I keep telling myself that we had insanely wonderful years together.

I'm just greedy.

I want more.

I know we did everything we could and spent every moment together. I had everything I - or anyone else- could want in marriage. Total love, commitment, fun, sex, fidelity, sharing, friendship, intimacy, conversation, non-stop conversation, a child.

I had it all, and should rejoice in that.

But I miss you. I want you here for another year, or five, or ten. We were cut short. We were happy, loving life, living life, and it ended. I really had it in my head. At seventy-eight or seventy-nine you'd start to slow down. That's when it happened with my parents. That would have – should have - been normal. Not seventy-two. Not last year.

It was too soon to leave us. A year before we celebrated twenty-two. A week before Kate's graduation. Way before I was ready. My guy friends all say you went out on top. They like that. You were happy, healthy, had great sex, and then it was over. No suffering, no lingering malady, not like dad, where it took months to die. Whammo. It was over. I guess I should be grateful for that. For all we did. For all we shared. For the twenty-five years we had together.

It doesn't make it any easier. It doesn't make the day less important. It doesn't make me miss you any less.

But when I walked to the tube today, I was telling you I miss you. I miss my travel buddy. And this enormous tourist bus pulled up on Baker Street with "RODGER'S" with a "D" on it. I had to laugh.

Coincidence?

I think not.

No gold Cadi, but you were telling me you were still around. That's what I choose to believe.

At Camden I saw all my antique guys. One who remembered me gave me a book as a gift.

The Magic of Love.

How apropos.

I love you, honey.

Happy anniversary.

ප

My last night of vacation.

I did it.

I traveled for almost two weeks on my own, without you, without any backup, without my guy. I visited all our favorite haunts. I wrote a lot, cried a lot, and walked a lot.

It was a nostalgia trip, but also a trip for my soul.

I can go on. I don't want to, but I can. In all my overweight, overstuffed suitcases, I bought a necklace and two pairs of shoes for me. The rest is for family and friends. This really is my purpose now. I can't think about me too much. I can't think about me without you. But the kids need me. Kate needs me. So I go on. And buying for friends and family makes me happy.

What I really want is for you to be here with me.

London and Paris were ours.

You with me the whole trip. I had your ashes with me, guiding me, protecting me, keeping me going. The only crisis was that I totally missed my "Love Never Dies" ticket. I thought it was for Saturday and it was Friday night. No biggie. I just bought another ticket. You always said when you travel you're going to get screwed at least once; just hope it's less than $100. And it was, almost.

I was terribly sad Friday night anticipating our anniversary and I blew it. But then I actually got to see the play *on* our anniversary, which I'll never forget.

Because you and I both know, love never really dies.

Paris changed me.

I was happy there, even lighthearted at times, filled with the burgeoning spring, my freedom, my memories.

Some of the shroud of sadness that hung on me has lifted.

I will always mourn.

I will always miss Rodger.

But he was so much a part of my experience there, in every step, on every corner, in every memory, I didn't miss him quite as much, because he was with me the whole time.

I came back with renewed energy. Someone said I look rested. Someone said I looked thinner.

What I was really, was at peace.

I learned that I could do something for me. Could go for a week without having to take care of the world. Without worrying about the office, my mother, the bills, the kids. It was all there when I came back, but I came back a different person. One who was less stressed, less tired, less weighed down by grief.

On that trip I found a part of *me* that has been missing all these months. The part that is hopeful, joyful, ready to grab life again and live it.

I can hear Rodger saying to me, "Go for it, Mary Kathleen."

So I am.

Whatever it is that this year will bring, I'm ready.

The kids went through Rodger's closet tonight. They were all in town for a baby shower.

A new life.

An end to an old life.

The boys are various ages and sizes, but they each found something in the closet they wanted. For Doug it was Rodger's old Frey boots he wore when they were growing up. Their old BB gun.

For Bruce, the luxury car dealer, it was a Ferrari sweatshirt.

Vik took an antique compact that belonged to her grandmother.

Katie was taken by an i.d. bracelet that said Rodger Sterling.

For Marc, closest in size to his dad, it was sweaters and sport coats.

And out of the pockets of all those old coats, all the suits, all the shirts, came the two things that identified Rodger Sterling.

There were pockets upon pockets full of business cards - Rodger Sterling, Editor, *Valley News Group*.

And there were a handful of matches from various pockets, from various places around the world.

The Diplomat Hotel in Prague. Sherlock's on Baker Street, London.

Cunard Line - the QE2 trip we took where we waltzed naked together in our stateroom.

They emptied the pockets and all my memories onto the desk. When the kids left I looked at the detritus and thought, "Damn, we had a good life."

And he would have been so thrilled to see the kids each claim something for their own. Some memory that resonated with them. Some piece of their dad they wanted to keep.

He would have been thrilled that they all showed up for Marc and Nicole. For the new baby. For the first Sterling boy in thirty-six years.

They celebrated the new.

And honored the old.

≥●

Back to reality. But a very much altered reality.

I wake up some mornings and think, "let's go for it." But after some teasing and touching nothing happens, so I figure I should just get up and unload the dishwasher.

But the Friday after I returned home from Paris I woke randy and ready.

I looked at Rodger's picture, thought about him, fantasized about him, fantasized about quite a few things, got myself turned on and came.

Twice, thank you.

I was obviously very happy when I got up and started my day, and then stopped in my tracks with a huge realization.

I didn't cry.

This is the first time in months that I haven't cried after I've come.

I don't know what it was about the trip. But I'm so much more centered. I no longer feel that half of me is missing. I feel that Rodg is with me all the time now. It's a very different state of consciousness. I'm lighter and freer.

I still cry for him. I still want him back. But I think I've entered a stage of acceptance that was a long time coming. It's almost been a year.

It still hurts, but it's no longer raw.

ै♪

The jacket still smells faintly of sweat, of travel, of Rodger.

I keep it under his pillow, on his side of the bed. I no longer cling to it every night, but touch it as a talisman, a reminder of what once was.

They say that smell is our strongest memory, and when I need to remember, when I'm blue, I'll hold it to me and try to smell him, bring him back. And try to remember the good times.

All the travels we had following that jacket down narrow European streets, into little cafes, in and out of funky hotels, onto trains for the next adventure.

Sometimes I'll throw it over a pillow, and hold onto that, pretending that he's still there, sleeping next to me, filling the jacket, filling the hole that's still in my heart.

But almost a year later, most nights I can sleep through without dreams, without sobs, moving into the next day.

I don't cling to the jacket every night.

It's no longer a lifeline.

It's a comfort.

Sometimes when I'm in a funky mood, I'll Google Rodger Sterling.

I have to be careful to put in the "D" and Woodland Hills or else I get the guy from the TV show "Madmen."

That was you, once upon a time.

You were the first "Roger Sterling" of ad agency fame, dealing with Lee Iacocca and John deLorean in a Detroit ad agency in the 60's. But when I Google-image you, the picture from your obit comes up. The one of you holding the newspapers in the park. That's you.

And I have to remind myself you were here.

You were real.

It was all real.

Because sometimes it's too far away. Sometimes it's like it's not real at all. That I didn't go through all that at the hospital. That I'm not living a life alone. The picture brings you into focus. My love, my life, my guy.

There on the Internet for all to see, but only for me to really know.

꧁

My goal now is to spoil people - children, grandchildren, friends.

Life is a lot simpler. I don't need much myself.

I no longer get letters from the market thanking me for being one of their top customers. I don't entertain as often. I don't need new clothes. I don't need another car. I'm spending my money and time on other things.

What I'm concentrating on now are the people who mean the most to me.

I went down to San Diego to be with the kids. I loved just hanging with them, taking them to dinner, buying birthday gifts and reveling in my new role as matriarch.

I know I don't need to spend money for them to love me. I *want* to spend money because I have it, they need it and it makes me happy. I can never fill the void of their father, but I can make their lives with new babies and new homes a little easier.

I also feel closest to Rodg when I'm with them. They miss him so much, and let me know it. It's okay to talk to them about him. We eat, drink, tell Rodger stories, and laugh. We remember the great things we did when they were younger. We talk about what they're doing now. They give Katie a hard time about college, about partying, living up to the Sterling name. We talk about the baby who's almost two, and the new baby on the way. It's all about family, and he's still a part of it.

There's a great picture on Marc and Nicole's mantle of Rodger making his toast at their wedding. His hand is almost coming out of the picture, holding his wine glass while he fetes the new couple. I can't stop staring at it while I'm there.

He is so vibrant, so happy for the kids, so alive in the picture

He's doing what he did best. Toasting life, toasting a wedding, toasting family. And all weekend he seemed to be reaching through the glass and toasting me.

Telling me to keep going.

To keep living.

To keep raising a glass to - and with - his kids.

Kate's come home.

She's here to write a paper quietly away from the dorm. It's wonderful to have her, whatever the reason.

We went to dinner last night at our favorite French restaurant. We talked and talked and talked about school, roommates, finding an apartment for next year. We caught up on family gossip, old friends we found on Facebook and more. We talked a little about Rodger and the kids, but not too much.

I sleep better when she's tucked in her own little room. My girl is home safe and sound.

I love that she's only an hour away and can drive down whenever she feels like it. I'm not so isolated. I'm not so alone.

Today she'll work on her paper, we'll make lunch.

Tomorrow maybe breakfast out and then a movie.

Right now there's laundry everywhere, and books piled on the coffee table. A computer and cell phone charger are plugged in at various places. There's a blanket on the sofa and dishes in the sink.

It's more than nice.

It's normal.

I haven't been this happy in months.

I'm going to work on taxes while she does her paper. No need to go out for anything else.

So I won't see a Cadillac today.

And I'm okay with that. I don't need that reassurance. I have her - and so much of Rodger in her.

It's a big step for me.

No security blanket.

No sad songs.

No looking for signs.

There's no need today. I have everything I could possibly want.

Right now, right here.

Breinigsville, PA USA
14 April 2011
259800BV00002B/1/P